HOLY HUMAN

Stories of Extraordinary Catholics

HOLY HUMAN
Stories of Extraordinary Catholics

Dick Ryan

Resurrection Press
An Imprint of
CATHOLIC BOOK PUBLISHING CO.
Totowa • New Jersey

Acknowledgment is gratefully given to the following newspapers and magazines where the stories originally appeared. They would include *Newsday,* the *New York Daily News,* the *New York Post,* the *National Catholic Reporter, Our Sunday Visitor,* the *Brooklyn Tablet* and the *American Catholic.*

First published in March, 2004 by
      Catholic Book Publishing/Resurrection Press
      77 West End Road
      Totowa, NJ 07512

ISBN 1-878718-89-4
Library of Congress Catalog Card Number: 2003115774

Cover design by Beth DeNapoli

Printed in the United States of America

1 2 3 4 5 6 7 8 9

Dedication

To my wife, Pat who, in a moment of weakness 45 years ago, showed her humanity by saying yes. And in all that time, with her patience, her easygoing nature, her love of family and (did I mention?) her patience above and beyond, she certainly qualifies as holy. And not even Shakespeare could find all the right words to describe what she has brought into my life and the lives of her children and friends with her presence, her gentle grace and her love.

Contents

Acknowledgments

I GUESS I started writing this book back in 1957 when Don Zirkel, then the editor of the *Brooklyn Tablet*, asked me if I'd like to try my hand writing stories about local Catholics who, in very ordinary ways, were very extraordinary people. And another chapter was written a few years later when Sal Gerage, the City Editor at the *New York Daily News* ("the skinny Victor Mature" as he called himself) extended the same invitation. But this time the stories and columns would be about everyone from politicians, ballplayers and businessmen to Willie Sutton, the bank robber and Dorothy Day, the saint.

And as the years went by, there would be other editors like Ed Wilkinson, Gerry Korson, Tom Roberts and Noel Rubinton who, with some amusement, read my stuff, shook their heads and eventually figured some way to send it off to print. My gratitude will always be there for their patience, their sense of humor, their high threshold of tolerance and their friendship.

It was through all of them that I was able to meet and interview all of the people in this book outside of my family, all of the people from Blessed Mother Teresa to Paul O'Dwyer to Bob Golden and Peter Clavin, undertaker, all of the people who in anyone's book, are some of the good guys of this world. They are people who came into my life as the focus of a story, an assignment, but who, in so many ways, touched a nerve that transcended anything that I could ever put down on paper about any of them. They are the good guys. Always will be.

It has been a special grace in my life, for instance, to sit down with someone like Marty Lyons, the ex-Jet football player, and instead of talking about touchdowns and tackles, chatted long into the afternoon about the children that he reaches out to in their final days.

There was also the day that I spent driving around the Bronx with Sister Lauria Fitzgerald as she gave out food to as many homeless people as she could find and those other days with the late Cardinal John O'Connor who, for all the times that he lashed out at politicians and pundits, was as down-to-earth and witty as most of my old uncles.

Add in Bill Flynn, Mike Piazza, Agnes Nixon and others and there is a rainbow of honesty, decency and humanity that put all of them, simply and unpretentiously, into a special bracket in my memory of each one of them when, not so long ago, I first met them.

Without brandishing rosaries or quoting St. Augustine in every lunch-time conversation, each of them, in his or her own way, is quite holy. Whether it is in taking their sense of morality and integrity into a boardroom or out onto a baseball diamond, they have the character and instincts that reflect an awareness of the presence of God in their work and in their lives and that defines an intestinal link to holiness that we never really associate with big business, sports or some half-hour soap opera.

In the same sense, they are all very human in the way that each of them lives in a knock-around world and recognizes some of the grime and grizzle all around them that are part of life but that are also the only available path to a higher and better place.

But none of their stories would have appeared inside the cover of this book if it weren't for my daughter, Tricia, who, with the patience of her mother, helped this stubborn illiterate wade his way through the ABC's of the computer. And there has to be a special thanks also to another daughter, Erin, and her husband, Roger, for all their help in making sure there was a quiet corner in their house where, for several months, I could manage to put it all down on paper, away from phones and television and the stern, not so serene "dinner's on the table!" echoing from the kitchen.

And finally, add the name of Emilie Cerar to the growing list of good guys in my life. The editor at Resurrection Press, Emilie patiently read through the maze of copy, made all the necessary revisions, suggestions and corrections and somehow nudged me through it with unflappable calm and that sweet, soft-spoken Emilie way. She fits in perfectly with all those in this book who, in so many different ways, so naturally and so generously touched my life in ways that soar far beyond nouns and verbs and adjectives.

Foreword

WHEN I read these profiles I picture myself sitting across a table from Dick Ryan in a coffee shop in Queens. I'm drinking tea—black as midnight on a moonlit night and he's drinking coffee with cream and sugar. With other journalists I might have to endure a bar in Manhattan. Now, however, I'm back in my kind of neighborhood. Outside it's a lovely day, either late spring or early autumn. Kids of every color under heaven are walking home from school in Catholic school uniforms. There's traffic on the street but it's not heavy. Occasionally, a squad drives slowly by. While we are waiting two young cops, one man, one woman come in for a "cuppa." I note with interest that they pay for it.

Through it all Dick spins his yarns. I conclude that he is a *seanachie*, an Irish storyteller telling stories about the United States, about the Catholic Church and above all about New York. Since I am from the second city I'm not exactly a New York fan, though out here it does not seem dissimilar from many neighborhoods in Chicago. I suspend my Midwest chauvinism and let the colors and the tone and the style of his stories flow through my veins. In a world where these kinds of stories can be told and read by millions of people, there is still hope for humankind.

So, gentle reader, imagine yourself in a similar spot, relax, prepare yourself for a good time and listen.

—*Andrew Greeley*

Part I

History's Unlikeliest Heroes

What, Me Fast?

THERE was a time last year when we were well into Lent and, bless me, Father, I hadn't done much fasting. And I wasn't alone.

But a lot of people, young and old, don't even think about it because they fast all year. They're either on a diet or they're very careful about what they eat. So jumbo cheeseburgers and chocolate mousse are never on their menu. Besides, a lot of otherwise devout Christians have discovered that fasting doesn't have to include a knife and fork.

For instance, some people fast from television for the forty days while some women, saints all, fast from their beloved shopping binges and weekends at the mall. Still others fast from smoking and the usual rounds of Happy Hours and the world can only hope that there are a few reformed souls out there fasting from their cell phones in the car or in their mezzanine seat at the theater.

But if I really wanted to observe Lent in a way that isn't just a contest with the refrigerator, I would fast from things like sarcasm and criticism. Sarcasm in every conversation. Criticism of people I don't even know. I might also think about fasting from snide asides about people who don't look like me or sound like me.

Actually, there is a whole litany of things that I would try fasting from if only I had a smidgen more of will power. Things like jealousy, temper, a terminal case of laziness, the daily blather of gossip and the stubborn old grudges that never die.

But right now, in this country and at this time in history, the only thing that I might really want to think about is a fast from fear. Fear of the unknown. Fear of dying. Fear of old age. Fear of terrorism. Fear of an uncertain future and an unnerving present. Fear of all the things that we can't control but are still out there spooking us and crowding in on us so that we're afraid to move and become all the things that should complete us.

Fear came shattering in on all of us on September 11th a few years ago and it roared in again a year later when Father Larry Penzes, a Catholic priest, was crucified by a bullet on his own Long Island altar, two weeks before Good Friday. The passion and death of the Easter legacy was never more chilling or more frightening.

Everyone in the church that day still remembers all of it but they still cling fiercely to the belief that, after Good Friday, there is always Easter Sunday when the stunning realities of faith and hope tower over violence, hatred and every conceivable fear.

Fear swallowed up that first Good Friday but Easter Sunday spit it out for the ages just as it still always rises above all the angers, jealousies and fears that, fasting or not, eat us up.

As he lay bleeding on his altar, just under the crucifix, Father Larry Penzes left the eloquently wordless message by his life—and death—that, with faith, there can be no fear.

∞

How do you handle the fears that are so much a part of life in the 21st century?

Angel Over Auschwitz

"HE could not be influenced by anyone when he was doing something that he thought was right," remarked 86-year-old Emilie Schindler as she talked about her late husband, Oskar, the German Catholic industrialist who, several years ago, was the center of Steven Spielberg's classic film, *Schindler's List*. "And he had a great ability to influence others. He had courage, and it took great courage to do what he did."

As a Catholic, was he an especially spiritual man? "He was a believer," she smiled softly, looking across at the man who was interpreting her German for the visitor asking the questions.

"By the war's end," a *New York Times* film critic wrote when the film was first released, "Schindler, who was by no means a saint, had bartered his vast fortune to save 297 Jewish women and 801 Jewish men reported to be on his list of workers. Years later, he died virtually penniless."

He was not a fanatic and he was not a saint so what kind of man was Oskar Schindler who saved more than a thousand Jewish lives during the Holocaust and went on to live a life of relative obscurity before his death in 1974. Some accounts describe him as a charming, partying, wheeler-dealer rogue who was never very bashful around women and was also a member of the Nazi Party during his peak as a successful businessman in occupied Poland. He made money on the black market and, at six feet four inches, was an imposing figure whether he was standing around chatting with the Schutz-Staffel (SS) or striding through his factory.

But he had no way of knowing how his life would be changed forever by the events that would spill out across World War II as that horrific time in history known as the Holocaust. Soon after the Nazis took over Poland, Schindler set up an enamelware factory in Krakow that produced kitchen equipment for the German army. And right next to it, he built a work camp known as Emalia where he employed hundreds of Jews. The working conditions under Schindler were far more humane than those experienced by the Jews confined to Plaszow, a Nazi labor camp that was also near Emalia.

Toward the end of the war, with the approach of the Russian army, Plaszow was shut down and Schindler was ordered by the Nazis to close Emalia as well so that the Jewish workers could then be shipped off to places like Auschwitz and the other Nazi death camps.

Suddenly aware of the possible fate of his workers, Schindler persuaded the Nazis to let him open a special munitions factory at Brinnlitz in Czechoslovakia. When they agreed, Schindler then compiled a list of over a thousand Jewish men and women who—he again convinced the Nazis—were essential to the war effort and the success of the factory.

Thus, "Schindler's list" was engraved forever in history. And so also were the *Schindlerjuden*, the names on that list who were eventually saved by Schindler. One of them was a man named Abraham Zuckerman who, years later, became a successful businessman in New Jersey.

"I was only 18 when I was sent to the Plaszow camp and then moved to Schindler's Emalia," recalled the 68-year-old construction executive who, over the years, has renamed countless New Jersey streets in honor of Oskar Schindler. Standing nearby in a crowded New York ballroom of people who had come together to pay tribute to the memory of her late husband and, indirectly, promote his movie, Emilie Schindler listened intently as he spoke.

"He was there with us, overseeing things, a very friendly, outgoing man," Zuckerman continued. "Before I came to Emalia, I was in four other camps and was sure, a hundred percent, that I was going to die. But Schindler was always right there, in the fire, surrounded by the Nazis. He was an angel. What else can I say?"

And the turning point for Schindler, from a free-wheeling, hard-nosed business hustler to a fearless savior of human life? He once confided to one of the *Schindlerjuden* that "in the beginning, I was working for the Nazis. But when I saw the killing of innocent people, I became their enemy."

There was one especially chilling incident that Schindler always remembered about Plaszow. Two young Jewish girls who had escaped were captured and then hanged. The camp's commandant, leaving nothing to chance, pulled out his gun and shot both of them as they hung there. When Schindler saw that, he walked away and vomited.

Later on, when over 300 women were mistakenly shipped out to Auschwitz and certain extermination, Schindler got into his car and drove to the notorious death camp where thousands of Jews were murdered every day. There he bribed the commanding officer and had the women sent back, unharmed, to Brinnlitz.

Sol Urbach was only 15 when he met Schindler for the first time. The Nazis had rounded up over a hundred Jews and brought them to Schindler to work in his factory. When Schindler saw Urbach in the crowd, he turned to the Nazi commandant and, with gruff sarcasm, shrugged, "you have children here?"

"You better keep what we deliver," the Nazi responded with a sneer.

"Some time later," Urbach recalled, "the SS sent a death squad into the Krakow ghetto where my family lived and slaughtered everybody. But Schindler, hearing about it, kept us in the factory until it was all over. As it was, I lost my parents as well as my three brothers and two sisters."

Later, Schindler saved Urbach again when he placed his name on his list as one of the "essential" workers for his bogus munitions factory in Brinnlitz.

"He was a savior," Urbach said quietly. "I saw him a number of times in Germany after the war and later on in Jerusalem. He was a man who took a lot of risks and saved a lot of lives. There was no one like him."

"To this day, I have no idea what made a man like Oskar Schindler do what he did," added Murray Pantirer, a 68-year-old survivor and one of the people on Schindler's list. "Why would he bother with people like us? We were nothing to him. And yet, he lost his business and all his wealth taking care of us and buying us food. For all the time I knew him, he was a great statue of a man, someone who enjoyed a good time and liked seeing others enjoy life. I was only one of seven children who survived, so you can see that Oskar Schindler was like an angel who flew down to save us. And in the end, he lost absolutely everything.

"I'll tell you one thing, he was a tremendous human being. He could have walked away and left us at any time, but he never did. As long as we were there, he was there with us, and he didn't have to be. And he gave us back something that we had lost—hope."

No fanatic and no saint, Oskar Schindler merely rescued over twelve hundred Jews from the worst kind of atrocities and certain death. And he did it with cool, uncompromising courage as he witnessed, up close, human beings slaughtering other human beings. As Emilie Schindler said so simply that day in New York about this unusual man who was honored in Israel in 1961 as a Righteous Gentile, "he believed."

"I'm one of those who survived, thanks to the Schindlers," remarked Moshe Beisky, a former Israeli Supreme Court judge. "To this day, I preserve the image of Mrs. Schindler bringing us pots of soup that she cooked herself with food that she got at great risk at the black market."

A few weeks after we talked in that packed ballroom, Emilie Schindler went to Jerusalem where she received a medal that earlier had been presented to her late husband. The simple inscription on the medal is a sentence from the Talmud and it eloquently summed up the lives of Oskar and Emilie Schindler, as well as the lives of all those names that were scribbled down, once upon a time, on Schindler's list: "whoever saves a single life is as one who saved an entire world."

The life and heroic efforts of Oskar Schindler will probably never be recorded in the official lives of the saints but across a few searing years during a terrible time in history, he saved a small, hallowed part of the world that will enshrine forever his footprints and the echo of his tough, gallant heart.

∽✕∾

What part did Schindler's faith play in saving so many lives?

Fathers and Sons
and Paul O'Dwyer

THIS Irish father had always worried, senselessly, about his children. He had always fretted, with black, brooding melancholy, that he would somehow have to live until he was 98 to make sure that all his children would be raised with the fewest cavities and the fewest hang-ups, with all the bills paid and all the cupboards filled and the utmost assurance that all of them would live happily ever after.

This Irish father was, of course, a worrier and he knew it. And only once in a while did he allow himself the luxury of looking ahead to the future through the more robust tissues of the Irish soul. The side that understands words like struggle and survival and, in all of it, scoffs at the scars and somehow always manages that warm, sweet taste of hope in his throat and the small, sly glint of victory in his wink. And that was why, some years ago, this Irish father treated his two oldest sons, Tom and John, to lunch with another Irish father so they could glimpse, up close, the more indomitable edges of the Irish soul in Paul O'Dwyer.

It was just coming into the afternoon when the Irish father, his two sons and Paul O'Dwyer slid into the corner booth of a restaurant just around the corner from Paul's Wall Street law offices. The boys, 19 and 18, had heard more than a little from their father about the man from County Mayo and Tom had even recently finished reading his autobiography, *Counsel for the Defense*. But John had come not really knowing what to expect, not completely aware of what would make this one so different from all the other Irishmen who eventually found their way into his father's home.

And now as the boys picked at their salad and asked a few awkward questions of the man with the bushy eyebrows and thick mane of white hair, O'Dwyer began talking in that crisp, clear Bohola brogue about politics and people, about his days in City Hall and down south during the civil rights marches of only a few years before.

He was just warming up as he began talking about his time in Fort Worth defending five men accused of illegal gun-running and about another time when he sat across the breakfast table with the redoubtable leader of so many subway strikes, Mike Quill. He also talked about his days, more recently, in Iran not only fighting his case against the former Shah of Iran for the billions of dollars that the Shah had taken with him into exile but also pleading his case with the Iranian honchos for the release of the hostages who were being held. O'Dwyer had obviously not spent the last few years planning his golden years or coddling a nine-iron on some suburban golf course.

But somewhere between the London broil and the coffee, O'Dwyer started talking about his own children, about the red hair of one of them that is so much like Tom's and John's, about his own childhood in Ireland and the hospital that he founded years ago in his Mayo hometown to care for the crippled and the severely handicapped so as to "give something back to the town that raised me."

As he talked and the two boys listened with surprising, spellbound awe, I was reminded about another Irish father, from another time, who never really talked that much about his younger years in Ireland or his introduction to New York City as the Depression was just beginning to swallow up the country. I was reminded of this thin, spindly little man who was born in County Carlow and who, with my mother, raised three of us in a city where people like O'Dwyer and Mike Quill and so many cops and bus drivers and iron workers set a gritty example for the immigrant Irish and all those who had come here with a dream and some Gaelic fantasy about gold flowing in the streets.

And as O'Dwyer leaned over, as intently as he might have looked across the table at a civil rights hearing, he began to ask

Tom about his plans after Fordham and John about some of his dreams as a young, born-again Irish-American.

And I thought again about the thin little Irish father who loved to talk to us about school and our visit "out in the country" in Brooklyn with Aunt Catherine and Uncle Neville. I remembered how he liked to sing "Kevin Barry" when the company came and the beer and whiskey flowed like the River Liffey and I thought of all those times when this frail little frame of my father trudged down 83rd Street after a long day at work, the *Daily News* and *Daily Mirror* tucked under his arm before climbing the four flights of stairs before supper and then all the doom-and-gloom news from Gabriel Heatter on the radio.

Suddenly, it was all over as Tom and John watched O'Dwyer finish his coffee and wave to a few people walking by. But the other Irish father at the table couldn't leave it at that. He wanted to preserve some deathless moment from the afternoon, some eloquently spontaneous quotation for posterity and his sons' memory of the occasion.

"Paul," I asked with measured gravity, "looking back at your own childhood in Ireland and your experience here as a father with your children and grandchildren, what would you say is the strongest, finest quality of the Irish father?"

"The strongest, finest quality of the Irish father," O'Dwyer responded just as gravely, choosing his words with slow, deliberate precision, "is that he leaves it all to the Irish mother."

O'Dwyer's laughter exploded with an instant, uproarious wail as the three of us followed in its infectious wake. He had pounced on the clumsy straight line. He had gotten a kick out of his own humor while turning the humor in on himself. And the boys saw another side of the man that complemented so many other things about him, some of his humility and humor, some of the dimensions of the man that were not always that visible on a face that only hinted at his cheery toughness and the blunt honesties and loyalties that simmered beneath.

And these, of course, had always been the badge and beauty of Paul O'Dwyer right up to the moment when he died a few years ago. He never tired. He never stopped caring about the worst of us, or the least of us. He was generations ahead of prophets and priests in his concerns for the black and the defenseless and in his opposition to something as murderous and senseless as war. And he said it. Said it right out there, plump and loud, when even senators and cardinals were playing it safe and discreet and silent. Set him so far apart from so many of the others, from the politicians , from the Irish who sometimes try so hard to be Protestant, from all those who hated him because he talked out, so passionately and so forcefully, about some of the things in the deepest recesses of our souls that shame us all.

And now as Paul O'Dwyer walked back to his office, his arm around Tom's shoulder, John walked behind with his Irish father, the two of us talking about the food and the Mets and this man O'Dwyer. And as we shook hands with him at the corner and he walked away, there was the strange eery feeling that the three of us were walking to the subway with another smaller, frailer man tagging along beside us. Another Irish father shuffling along with the three of us, the *News* and *Mirror* under his arm, and the soft, sweet sound of Kevin Barry floating across the street and filling the warm summer air.

☙✖❧

Whose stories do your children need to hear?

The Gospel According to Chavez

IF you had seen him on the street or in the subway, you might have mistaken him for a cabdriver or an unemployed waiter from one of the downtown restaurants. But here with a plain sports shirt and an old pair of cotton pants, and in a roomful of priests, Sisters and ministers from all across Brooklyn and Queens, he was the center of attention and the guest of honor in the summer of 1974 for an early morning clergy breakfast where the theme was "Together for Justice."

There were the usual red and black banners and the photographs of all these faces working in the fields under a scorching California sun. The dais included people like Rabbi Chaim Etrog, Reverend Grant Anderson, Sister Margaret Smyth and Father Bob Kennedy from Catholic Charities. Bishop John Snyder completed the prestigious group and sat next to this pleasant, ordinary looking man whose smile, gentle and genuine, was not the plastic grin of the politician that salivates over a seat on any dais but rather the serene expression of someone who was able to electrify a room just by walking through the door.

Cesar Chavez had come out to the auditorium at Our Lady Queen of Martyrs in Forest Hills to talk about lettuce and grapes and Gallo wine, nothing especially deep or theological for this group. He had come out to talk about the men, women and children who were working on the farms of California where a glass of water was one of the luxuries of the day.

When Bishop Snyder stood at the microphone, only a subway ride away from the black-tie grandeur of the Waldorf Astoria, he welcomed Chavez on behalf of Bishop Francis Mugavero and the entire Brooklyn Diocese. He then began talking about the struggles of Cesar Chavez and his farmworkers and, with crisp, cliché-free simplicity, he expressed the hope that Chavez and his people would soon find that same justice, dignity and freedom that this country celebrated the week before on July 4th.

Then it was Cesar Chavez's turn to talk, and for the next half hour, this short, stocky man talked about the workers' strike and the non-violent boycott that he and the farmworkers had been waging all across the country and about the kind of brutal, daily atrocities that, for the American middle-class, "eye has not seen, nor ear heard . . . ."

He talked also about one of the wine companies earning more than forty four million dollars the year before while he and his workers had to fight with the growers to have separate toilet facilities installed in the fields for the women. He talked about the farmworkers having to drink water from an old rusty beer can and about the thousands of children who had died before they could write their names because they had spent too many nights in dirty, smelly shacks where there was little food and no toilets, bath tubs or running water. He then talked about the day two of the workers were shot to death in an open field and life going on as usual. He talked about all of this and suddenly the buns and orange juice on the tables were tasteless and sour.

And at the end of his talk, Chavez thanked the priests and all the others for coming out and, hopefully, bringing his message back to their parishes and their schools. The message that the United Farmworkers' lettuce is covered with cellophane and is stamped with a black eagle and that all the other lettuce is scab. He also suggested that all the wines produced in Modesto, California be left on the shelves.

Before leaving, he stood for a few minutes behind the dais with Bishop Snyder and some of the others who came over to shake his hand and wish him well. And in one of those moments when he was suddenly alone, I nudged my way through the crowd to ask him a question and simply meet the man.

How, I stammered, at another time and place, would he be able to convince a somewhat unfriendly crowd that was mostly unsympathetic to his boycott and his ideas?

"By the morality of it," he said quickly. "I am talking about men, women and children in the fields who are being exploited by the growers by a way of life that is buried in poverty, squalor and the kind of indignities that you couldn't imagine. If the immorality of this kind of treatment does not offend people, then nothing will."

I then asked him if he consciously related his daily work out in the fields to his life as a Christian and his relationship with God. "I am trying to do the same things that He tried to do, to feed the hungry, to clothe the naked, to give water to those who are thirsty. It is what we are all trying to do, and eventually we will. We are about the work of Christ on earth."

He smiled and shook hands and walked off the dais. The next stop would be Buffalo and then Albany, and then back to the Coachella Valley in California and his family in Delano. For sixteen hours a day and seven days a week, he had been walking into auditoriums like this one and then marching with his pickets outside the big supermarkets to convince as many people as possible about a message that was difficult for many to understand or appreciate.

He was trying to tell them, in precepts that were sometimes grating and repulsive, that the first and greatest commandment is to love Christ who, for Chavez, was a young Chicano girl forced to stand humiliated outside a common toilet. And the second greatest commandment is to love our neighbor who, for Chavez, was a tired, sunbeaten farmworker, old beyond his years, someone who probably wouldn't live past his fiftieth birthday, someone who dropped out of school to help his family, someone who never earned more than $1,575 in a year, someone who had watched thousands of children, undernourished and spindly, withering away in the fields and who stood by helplessly as his own wife and daughter were being subjected to the most shamefully obscene indignities imaginable.

He was trying to tell people that they were feeding the hungry when they refused to buy a head of non-union lettuce, that they were clothing the naked when they ate something else besides grapes, and that they were extending their hand to the poor and the outcast when they didn't buy their wine from certain companies based in California.

With their in-your-face buttons and banners and their throaty boycott, Cesar Chavez and his people were perhaps too close to both the streets and the earth itself for many of us to recognize the ties to people like Peter and John the Baptist charging in with fire in their eyes. So some of us instead snickered at the idea of picketing a supermarket or putting one of their bumper stickers on our car while we looked around for something a little more antiseptic, something with more incense-and-hymns in our religion. Something a lot safer and more politically correct than the gospel according to Chavez.

But to the very end, Cesar Chavez, with that crummy sports shirt and an old pair of cotton pants, trudged across the country and into the big cities with his plea, his challenge, his vision of what could yet be good and just and moral. And always, wherever he stood, wherever his voice sliced across the rain or scorching sun, there was always something in his words, and in his eyes, that was as old and troubling and beautiful as the Sermon on the Mount.

⚬⚭

Are boycotting and picketing a way for you as a Catholic to respond to injustice?

The Lullaby of Barbara

YOU have to understand, first of all, that what you are about to read would never see the light of day in any of your local gossips columns. And for a very good reason.

Gossip columns, the toilets of the press, prefer to deal in dirt, drivel and rumor. It's as simple as that. They delight in stories of tinsel-town cannibalism, celebrity divorce and all the other lurid scandals that are intended to bury the living and dishonor the dead. It is business-as-usual as they seasonally exhume the skeletons of Monroe, Dean and Presley as if they hadn't tortured them enough when they were alive. As writers, the gossip columnists are several notches beneath those sensitive souls who scribble all kinds of four-letter poetry on the walls of most bus terminal washrooms.

What it comes down to is that words like compassion, principle and charity never quite make it on their computers and that is why gossips have never quite been able to understand someone like Barbara Sinatra and what she has done so quietly with her life while in the eye of celebrity.

The widow of the late Frank Sinatra, this unobtrusively, soft-spoken, down-to-earth woman who came out of the small Midwestern town of Bosworth, Missouri has spent much of her life trying to make things a little nicer for the Bosworths of Senegal and Mauritania and the edges of the Sahara Desert.

At one time in her life, Barbara Sinatra was the vice president of an organization called the World Mercy Fund. And instead of simply going through the la-de-da motions of lending her 14-carat name or sending a check in the mail, she personally put in her time in the trenches for the work of the Fund in some of the poorest and dingiest corners of the map.

Over the years, for example, she has visited parts of Africa that are not usually recommended as vacation spots by your friendly travel agent. Accompanied there by Father Tom

Rooney, the founder of the World Mercy Fund, she has lived with the missionary Sisters, visited the sick poor and then returned later at another time to see what she could do, to put her fingers into the wounds, and then return to America to let the world know that, yes, there are thousands of people dying in Africa because they don't have a crust of bread or a glass of water.

"But even before you can help these people," she told me once, "you have to overcome their superstitions and their belief in witchcraft. I remember once seeing a little girl whose deformed hand had an extra thumb. But the child's mother refused to permit an operation on the hand because she felt it was the will of God so the little girl remained deformed to this day."

Mrs. Sinatra then recalled seeing a worm, almost a foot long, being removed from the stomach of a little boy only to see the mother insist on preserving the worm in a container because it was "what God wanted."

"There was another time," she remembered, "when I witnessed a young 15-year-old mother walk across the desert for about five hours, accompanied by her daughter, to fetch water. When she finally got it, she put it into a bucket, placed it on her head and walked back again. And the water was filled with all kinds of insects and filth."

A convert to Catholicism, Barbara Sinatra has never been far from a church wherever she has traveled. "Whenever Frank and I were in New York, he usually liked to go to St. Malachy's. But Father Rooney used to take me to the chapel of the Franciscan Medical Missionaries. But wherever I happen to be, Catholic churches have always afforded me with a certain sense of belonging. I've always felt that Catholics generally stand up for what they believe. It's like the nurses and nuns in Africa," she explained. "They go there and stay there because of what they believe.

"I feel that I've been very lucky all my life," she said suddenly. "I've had a healthy life, a wonderful husband, and yet there are so many others in the world who are less fortunate. And if we don't help them, where will they get it?"

And then, without anyone asking, Barbara Sinatra started talking about her late husband, proudly, warmly, affectionately. "I used to see him pick up a newspaper, time after time, " she said with a smile, "read an isolated story about a child or someone needing an operation or some other kind of help, and then immediately sit down and send out a check, and always anonymously."

And the benefits and concerts, year round, were something else. "As hard as my husband used to work," the former farm girl from Bosworth said with a slight twinkle, "he worked more for charity than for himself." And this was a sentiment echoed by Father Rooney when, at one time, he referred to Frank Sinatra as "the most generous man that I have ever met anywhere in my life." And that life took this gritty priest to just about every pocket on the globe.

Once upon a time in the fascinating life of this rather fascinating priest, Tom Rooney worked as a promising young engineer for the Shell Oil Company, traveling all over the world, from the West Indies to Baghdad and over to Singapore, exploring oil wells and polishing up the good life of a young man in a hurry.

But then one fine day, Rooney, who was born in Ireland, found himself transferred to Africa where he suddenly found himself knee deep in a level of poverty and human misery that he never believed possible in the civilized world. And it was during one of his trips to Nigeria that he came upon a 16-year-old girl lying at the side of the road with her unborn infant struggling to be born, a tiny hand protruding helplessly from its mother's womb.

So Rooney stopped his car, tried to deliver the baby and, when this was unsuccessful, helped the young girl into his car and took her to the hospital. Four miles along the road, a friend who had come along with him informed Rooney that it was too late, the girl was dead.

It was then, standing with his friend at the roadside grave that they had dug for the young girl, that Tom Rooney made the biggest decision of his life. He went back to England, turned in his resignation to Shell Oil and, four years later, was ordained to the priesthood as a Holy Ghost Father. And the rest, as they rarely tell you in the gossip columns, is history, incredible history.

Father Rooney, who has since passed away, went on to create the World Mercy Fund which, under his direction, and with the help of Barbara Sinatra, raised millions of dollars for Africa and other Third World countries. So that for almost six months of every year, he criss-crossed a couple of continents, personally distributed food, clothing and medical supplies and even helped plot out developmental projects for clinics and relief agencies of every religion and creed throughout the Third World. He was in Ethiopia trying to stem the tide eight years before the rest of the world realized the scope of that country's suffering.

In the first sixteen years of World Mercy's existence, Father Rooney built 82 clinics, 28 grade schools, four hospitals, two agricultural schools and a technical training school. And there was one year when, again with the help of Barbara Sinatra, they raised more than three and a half million dollars in their valiant crusade against poverty, hunger, disease, superstition and drought. In the bargain, Father Rooney contracted malaria a couple of times while Barbara shrugged off the hepatitis that she was stricken with during one of her trips to Africa.

But the hepatitis was nothing compared to some of the things that she had seen and that burned across her consciousness. A little girl with eleven fingers. A young teenage mother trudging across a sweltering desert with a bucket of dirty water as a special luxury for her child. The story of an open grave near an African roadside when a young Irish engineer stood for the first time with a vision of another time, another place, with young healthy mothers and strong, vibrant, living children.

"I've been very lucky," Barbara Sinatra said softly from her home in California as she thought about all those faceless millions that she and her old friend, Father Rooney, had literally traveled to the ends of the earth to help. All those countless, forgotten children whose only taste of pure water was that of their mothers' tears as they fell asleep at night.

♲

Have you ever missed the good works being done by others because of your shortsightedness and misjudgments?

The Improbable Saint:
New Yorker and Black

IF Pierre Toussaint is ever canonized as the first black American saint, there will be dancing in the streets from Harlem to Bedford Stuyvesant and, glory be, Saint Pierre might even replace Saint Patrick as the patron saint of New York. Faith and begorrah!

"He was a very holy man who reached out to help everyone who needed any kind of help, and it never made any difference to him about the color of the other person's skin," explained Monsignor Robert O'Connell, the vice postulator for Toussaint's cause and the pastor of New York's oldest church, St. Peter's in downtown Manhattan where Toussaint attended daily Mass for almost seven decades. He was no Reverend Al Sharpton or Reverend Jesse Jackson but, like most saints, he quietly let his actions leave their own eloquent message as his legacy.

Born into slavery in the French colony of Haiti in 1766, Toussaint was among the 800,000 slaves who made it easy for the French plantation owners to amass huge amounts of wealth from their coffee and sugar crops. But when the French revolution exploded and the slaves lashed out with their own uprising, many of the slave owners packed up and fled. And John Berard du Pithon, Toussaint's master fled to New York City with his wife, his sister, four slaves and Toussaint.

And when du Pithon fell on hard times in the city and eventually died, Toussaint stayed on with his master's family and, for the next twenty years, supported them with the money that he earned as a hairdresser. And even beyond that, Toussaint and his wife, Juliette, who was also a slave, made their modest home a haven for orphaned black children, raised them and eventually even found jobs for them. He also raised enough money (through his wealthy customers) for a special home for orphans that had been built by a priest and that helped those who needed food, medicine or clothing.

When, on her deathbed, his late master's wife arranged for his freedom, Toussaint dedicated the rest of his life, and much of his money, toward ransoming the freedom of other slaves. He also spent the lion's share of his time visiting and nursing those who had been struck down by yellow fever or cholera.

"Pierre Toussaint never bemoaned the fact that he had been a black slave," explained Monsignor O'Connell. "He loved freedom and personally ransomed the freedom of many slaves in his time. But his own slavery was never an issue for him, nor was it something that he talked about."

Pierre Toussaint died in New York City in 1853 at the age of 87 and, in a brief account of his life, Father B.M. Horton confirms Monsignor O'Connell's point about Toussaint's approach to the issue of race in those pre-Civil War decades. "He never spoke of slavery as an institution as far as we know," Horton wrote. "Once, when asked to lead a political parade on the issue, he refused, saying, 'they have not seen blood flowing as I have. They do not know what they are doing.'"

In reviewing Toussaint's life, however, both blacks and whites would readily agree that nothing seemed more personally important and critical to Toussaint than simply helping others—even his own slave masters.

As part of the process of canonization, miracles play no small part in the eyes of the Vatican. And there is already one instance where it seems a reality. A man in Haiti had been diagnosed in 1966 as having cancer in both the abdomen and lung. The story goes that a local priest who had been counseling the patient at the time suggested that he pray to a fellow Haitian, Pierre Toussaint. However, after the doctors operated unsuccessfully on the 25-year-old patient, they gloomily predicted that he had only about three more months to live.

While the patient continued to lose weight, hope and the will to live, the prayers to Pierre Toussaint continued. And when finally the doctors routinely examined the patient on one particular day, they found, to their amazement, that there wasn't a trace of cancer anywhere in the man's body and there wasn't a shred of medical explanation for any of it. He was pronounced completely healthy.

Undoubtedly, millions of Catholics will one day be venerating Pierre Toussaint as the first black American saint by way of the streets of New York. However, it will not be because he stormed the barricades of institutional racism or personally blockaded the entrances of bureaucratic chambers in a dramatic plea for better housing, bigger schools or more jobs. In today's climate of unrest and volatility, Toussaint may come to be seen as a sign of contradiction with his serenely thoughtful understanding of words like brotherhood and neighborhood and family.

He may also come to be eventually embraced as a model of simple, face-to-face human concern in its most fundamentally personal form. In that moment, he will be revered as the truest, purest reflection of real racial harmony in that the color of a person's skin was never a consideration in anything that he said or did. Toussaint was always quietly eloquent in living out a standard of Christianity that was uniquely courageous if only for its raw, gospel simplicity.

In many ways, he epitomizes New York. The tough times and all the nostalgia. And where it can yet soar.

⚮

What "quiet" saints do you personally know?

Saint Martin Luther King, Jr.?

WHEN, in the early part of 2000, the American bishops proposed that Pope John Paul II honor Dr. Martin Luther King, Jr. as a martyr during the Church's jubilee celebration that year, it was greeted in some corners of the Church as a dramatic cause for celebration among all blacks, both Catholic and non-Catholic. The more cynical shrugged it off with a tired yawn, viewing it as a nice gesture, slick public relations, a politically correct idea that really meant nothing.

But if the bishops and the Vatican were really sincere about including Dr. King in the august company of other martyrs such as St. Paul, Joan of Arc and countless others, then they might have taken the next logical step and added the word "saint" to his name since all martyrs are automatically considered as such throughout the long history of the Church.

Although nothing was ever officially declared about the one normally routine step into sincerity and credibility, it would have been a huge step forward in race relations for the Church since it is no secret that the issue of racism has never been the most comfortable issue in a Church that prides itself on its gallant crusades against abortion and euthanasia but too often reverts to "discretion" and silence when instances of racism flare up in their own dioceses and parish streets and in the privacy of a family kitchen.

But perhaps Dr. King's elevation as a martyr and an uncanonized saint might be greeted with spontaneous enthusiasm in the Church if there were more black priests and nuns in positions of prestige in the Church's chanceries where they could reach out to a broader audience of young blacks and relate the life of King and his pursuit of justice and equality to some of the messages in the pages of the gospel.

For whatever reason, the Church has never been very successful in recruiting young black men and women to its altars and its classrooms and then elevating them to positions of power. Devotion to St. Martin de Porres, a black saint, has always been a strong centerpiece of the black community so that special prayers to St. Martin Luther King, Jr. could multiply those numbers and broaden its base across the entire Church.

All too often, there has been a fence separating inner-city parishes from the suburban Church even though both listen quite attentively on Sunday when the priest utters those timeless, mechanical words about loving thy neighbor. All the more reason why the American bishops should indeed honor King as a martyr while also placing more emphasis, in their pastorals and public statements, about the need for a unified Church that could be, as never before, one, holy, catholic and universal as Dr. King always envisioned the someday bond between black and white in this country. It is for this reason that, while adding the word, martyr, to King's name, they might also include another word shared by so many of the Church's saints. Prophet.

If indeed the Church was serious and embraced Dr. King as martyr, saint and prophet, it would be seen as something much deeper and far more meaningful than a sly public relations stunt if it also added his name to the litany of saints recited at every Mass, declared January 17th as a Catholic feast day in his honor as well as a national holiday and finally declared him to be the patron saint of the powerless since he lived and died with the sole purpose of empowering all those on the edges of society and acceptance.

In reality, however, official canonization is turtle-slow across the pages of history. But no one can argue that, whether it happens in our lifetime or not, the life, death and message of this unusual man embodied every shred of hope and belief that are at the heart of the Catholic faith. He did indeed have a dream. The same one that was shared by another man who also died violently on a cross.

When in May of 2000, Pope John Paul II pronounced the name of Dr. Martin Luther King, Jr. as one of the great modern martyrs of the century, it was an opportunity for the Church to revitalize its efforts to reach out to every race and ethnic group and not stop short of simply engaging in a one-day pageant of pomp and praise that would fade away at the end of the day. While most of the country embraces the memory of this fearlessly courageous man every January, it might also be especially fitting if Catholics recalled the words of Pope John Paul II about Dr. Martin Luther King, Jr. who, in dying for justice, equality and the dignity of all men, added one more lustrous chapter to the Acts of the Apostles.

 exo

Would Catholics in your community accept Martin Luther King, Jr.'s recognition as a martyr or prophet?

The Cable Guy

"WE're moving into an era when 'grazing' will no longer be necessary for television viewers," Charles Dolan said somewhat prophetically in 1993 as he sat back at his desk in his Long Island Cablevision office. "In the future, watching television will be more directed and the menu will be driven by complete categories of programs appearing that day."

As the founder and chief executive officer of Cablevision and one of the most powerful players in the television industry, Dolan has been fascinated by communication ever since he began snapping photographs as a young Boy Scout in Cleveland and then selling them to a local newspaper. Shortly after that, he even began writing his own "column" for about $2 a week. With that, he was "hooked for life." And he has never stopped.

It was during the fifties when, after moving on from his precocious beginnings as a young Cleveland newspaper columnist, he began working for a company that supplied news to the networks, jumped over to Sterling Television and suddenly the steps got bigger and faster, and bigger still.

In 1961, Dolan founded the company that is now Manhattan Cable, the nation's first urban cable system, and then, ten years later, he established Home Box Office, the first premium service in the cable industry. And twenty years after he organized Cablevision in 1973, Dolan admitted modestly that it was the fifth largest in the country with over two million subscribers in nineteen states.

A devout Catholic with keen interest in helping the Church enter, and master, the information age, Charles Dolan has been a strong moral, and financial, supporter of Telecare, the television network of the Rockville Centre Diocese on Long Island. In fact, Telecare's director, Monsignor Tom Hartman vividly recalls the day in 1973 when, after six years on the air, Telecare was on the brink of shutting down.

Enter Charles Dolan who, without any bells or whistles, wrote out a check for $100,000 along with the promise of a guaranteed channel on his own cable network that would air all of Telecare's programs.

"Without Chuck Dolan," Hartman gushed recently, "we would have been finished. And he's been helping us ever since."

Dolan, however, is not pushy in giving either advice or his wealth of experience to Hartman or others in the Church who are in the business of spreading the word. In fact, he makes it a deliberate practice to blur the lines between his place in the pew and his prominence as one of cable's pioneers. And giants.

"Chuck once told me that we're selling the most important product of all on Telecare," Hartman revealed, "and that we shouldn't see the Church as a competitor to others on the screen, but rather as a service."

Dolan elaborated on that theme in a later interview, noting that the Church should be trying to shape the minds and hearts of television actors and producers and not trying to compete with them for a share of the ratings. "I'm not sure if the Catholic Church wants to come up with its own 'Roseanne' and challenge the big hits of the day," he began. "I would say, instead, that the Church would be more effective if it tried to reach one of the major stars on one of those programs, along with the people who produce it, and take it from there. If you can influence the leaders in the industry, that's important. It's not important that you try to compete with the hit show itself."

And asked what advice he would give to the nation's bishops concerning the use of television, his answer was crisp and immediate. "Stick to what you know best," he said without mincing words. "Educate and don't try to get into the ratings game. Don't worry about the size of the audience but just do it right, giving as much value to teaching as the Church has always done.

"Especially on some of those programs where current news is the focus. News is news so don't propagandize. Also, don't think that television is ready to replace the Catholic school. Television is a supplement to what's taught in the classroom and no more. But that's not to say that television isn't flexible and that creative people won't always find new ways to use it to its highest potential. There is no field today that is more challenging and with more rapid technological evolution."

Dolan noted also that the days are long gone when a Catholic prelate like the late Bishop Fulton J. Sheen could become a television "star" like he did during the '50s. "That was an era when personalities like the Bishop could succeed," Dolan said flatly. "People like Bishop Sheen dominated with their personal charisma and the public was interested. But today, the public isn't interested and that no longer works.

"And when you suggest that people like Reverend Jerry Falwell and other fundamentalist preachers on television are successful doing that kind of thing, I don't agree. I don't think they're reaching more than fifteen to twenty per cent of the audience. And besides, the same people listen to them all the time.

"In a sense, time is of the essence in television because you can't sit around forever," Dolan added, walking over to the window. "Otherwise, all the decisions will be made for you so that, whether you're producing a hit show or trying to bring the Church into the home, you better stay ahead of the game."

With programs that are still replete with "talking heads" and pious sermonettes, Catholic television still has a way to go in bringing "the Church into the home," in a way that is intelligent, creative and even entertaining. So it might not be the worst idea in the world to invite someone like Charles Dolan to take the reins nationally and spell out a formula for the bishops that goes well beyond one more yawning production of three people sitting around a table debating euthanasia.

It may not be *Frasier* or *60 Minutes* but, with Dolan in the room, it can only get better. Much better than it's been.

∽✕∾

What ideas do you have for making Catholic television relevant and interesting?

One Man's Declaration of (TV) Independence

"JUST call me Bill," the slender, shirt-sleeved man said breezily as he suddenly appeared in WNET's stately reception room and personally ushered me into his office. William F. Baker, polite and generous with his time, runs the largest public television station in the country, WNET/Thirteen which, in the bargain, serves the entire metropolitan New York area. Before I sat down, I gave him permission to call me Dick.

The conversation for the next forty-five minutes would be about public television, education and some of the things that have happened since Dr. Baker first walked into this office in 1986 as the new president and CEO of WNET/Thirteen. We didn't talk much about his birthplace in Cleveland or his Ph.D in Communications and Organizational Behavior and we didn't talk about his years as president of Group W Television with the Westinghouse Broadcasting Company before coming to WNET. Nor did we talk at all about any of the big networks that are into the business of selling, big-time, while WNET/Thirteen, Bill Baker tells you with dead-ahead eye contact, is into the stuff of service.

Sitting there and talking casually about a number of things. Baker has this deep, resonant radio voice that's been fine-tuned by years of training and on-the-air experience and that takes all of five seconds to put an audience in his pocket. But it's much more than a mellifluously cultured set of vocal chords that has pushed him to the head of the class. It's what's behind the beard and those piercing eyes and the trigger mind. It's what's cooking in there in his imagination and tightly organized mindset as Baker sits in his Manhattan office and talks about some of the things that interest a lot of us but that few of us ever get to change.

A few months earlier, I had sat in another larger room and listened as Bill Baker delivered a talk during an annual meeting of the TriState Catholic Committee on Radio and Television. His remarks to the audience were original and provocative as he talked about things like leadership and potential in the field of communications in the Catholic Church. An honest man with things to say and the nerve to say them, he didn't shy away from stepping on a few toes of those who felt they wrote the book about the medium and the message in the Catholic Church.

—"Our mission at WNET/Thirteen is to serve the public, not sell commercials. But as part of that choice, we have to raise a hundred million dollars every year."

—"If a cultural, educational institution like Channel 13 can't make it in New York, it can't make it anywhere."

—"I look for ethical and intellectual honesty in the people who come here to work. I don't hire people by how good they look or how smart they are."

—"When you look around at every other religion, the Catholic Church is only scratching the surface on television, and that's painful to me as a Catholic."

—"You have to understand that there is a clear separation between Church and State on television and, at WNET, we serve all faiths as well as unbelievers through our programs."

—"The Catholic Church can't present its values to the broader society unless it uses the electronic media and, in this regard, the Church has been very conservative and backward. It has not developed a broad strategic plan for television."

—"The bishops have not understood the media and, even if they've understood it, they haven't been comfortable with it. There are some who have understood but they haven't as yet utilized all the ability that's there."

—"The millions of dollars that the Church raises annually for communications is used wisely but it's hardly enough. We need millions of dollars a year at WNET alone and that's just one city. As Catholics, we have to give more so that the bishops can spend more."

Probably the most arresting quality about Bill Baker is that if you ask the man a question, you are going to get an answer. It may not be the answer you want or the kind of tempered, timid non-answer you may be accustomed to if you hang around politicians a lot, but Baker is invariably right from the shoulder, direct, blunt, no frills. And that may be the best reason why he, or someone like him, should be invited, begged, cajoled to advise and educate the Church about television and perhaps even head up a national committee of proven, respected television pros to develop "a broad strategic plan for television" and the Church.

When Baker first walked into the WNET/Thirteen headquarters in New York, there were a few left-over dreams and stubborn visions that were still floating around in the mind of this man whose parents never finished high school and who, in both the public and private sectors of television, has never settled for anything less than excellence, and the effort that goes with it.

"I've watched The American Dream come true in my own life," he said reflectively. "But in this job, I've finally found the one thing that, until now, had been missing. I can honestly say that, with this job and the challenges that go with it, I am a true public servant with an organization whose sole purpose is to serve the public. I think that the people at WNET can truly make a difference in television for every person and every segment of the community."

To understand anything at all about Dr. William F. Baker and the juices that drive him, farther and higher, than most of us, it's important, of course, to glean through some of his stunning professional achievements from his early days as an announcer at WGAR in Cleveland to his breakthrough years at Scripps-Howard Broadcasting and Westinghouse and finally to his current wave of success at WNET/Thirteen.

But there is something else. There is also this small, obscure footnote in there someplace in his bio that reveals he is one of only ten people in the history of the world to have climbed both the North and South Poles. That alone says something about his determination and his sense of risk. It also says something that is quite compelling about his courage and his dogged beliefs in his own gifts, his possibilities, himself. And it says something that Westinghouse and WNET/Thirteen and all the others have known all along about this daring, doing, talented man who has taken, and is still taking, a few bold steps in the direction of education and service to others that, unfortunately, the Church has approached ever so cautiously, or never really understood with the same passion and conviction of Bill Baker.

❧❀☙

Does your support of public television benefit the Catholic Church?

For Chris Burke, Life Goes On

ACCORDING to the medical textbooks, Down Syndrome is the most commonly occurring chromosomal abnormality, resulting when a person possesses three, rather than the usual two copies of the same chromosome. And every year in the United States alone, approximately five thousand children are born with Down Syndrome. A little over thirty-five years ago, Chris Burke was one of them.

But sitting in one of the conference rooms of the National Down Syndrome Society a few years ago, Burke talked about his work with the Society, his career as an actor on television, his family and his dreams. An extraordinary young man, he still travels around the country giving talks on Down Syndrome, is part of a three-piece band that has about 150 performances a year, has written a book and was in the process of completing a documentary. And if that's not enough to tire out most people, even considering his non-stop schedule, he is the first actor with Down Syndrome to star in a major prime-time television series. It was called *Life Goes On* and he managed to steal much of it as Corky Thatcher. And while the series is no longer on the air, life still goes on, quite happily, for Chris Burke.

For example, he still enjoys the time that he is able to spend traveling around the country speaking to different groups about his life and, indirectly, about the lives of those sitting there listening to him.

"I usually tell the audience that we never think of 'disability' in the Society but rather of 'ability'," he remarked while talking casually about his cross-country jaunts. "And that it's also important for those of us who have DS to be determined about what we are doing in life, and to never give up on anything. My mom always said that I'm a very determined person."

Chris considers himself as "sort of an ambassador for the National Down Syndrome Society "and he is never hesitant in expressing his thoughts about growing up with Down Syndrome. "I like talking to groups where there are children or where there are parents with children who have the same experience as myself," Chris added. "And no, I'm never nervous about speaking before large groups. It's just like when I'm acting and I'm told to do a certain scene. I just go ahead and do it."

Born and raised a Catholic, Chris has never allowed his busy schedule with the Society or in front of a television camera to get in the way of his faith. And it is something that he takes as seriously as all the other things that are such an intimate part of his life. "I'm actually a parishioner in two different parishes," Chris replied when someone asked him about his Sundays. "I attend both Epiphany Church on Manhattan's lower East Side and also Our Lady of the Miraculous Medal out at Point Lookout on Long Island where my family has a summer home. I usher there at the 5 o'clock Mass on Saturday nights. It's the same church where I was an altar boy when I was younger. But there's one other thing about being a Catholic. Aside from believing in God and the angels, I also believe in miracles, and that they can happen to anybody."

And does Chris Burke believe that the Church does enough to educate people about Down Syndrome and its relation to others in the parish and in society? His answer came without a blink of hesitation.

"I like the idea that parishes have both altar boys and altar girls who have Down Syndrome," he said. "I think that the Church does reach out to us and gives us a chance to serve in a house that is really God's house. There are people who are blind and there are people who are crippled but God is always telling us that miracles can happen in our lives. But he's also giving us a chance to be out in the world and not only do things for ourselves but also be able to make better things happen in the world."

The youngest of four children, Chris Burke has always placed his family at the top of the list whether he happens to be acting on television, speaking to a large PTA group in Peoria, spending time with his friends or putting the finishing touches on his documentary or one of the many other projects that are still on the drawing board and out there for him in the future.

"My family has always encouraged me," he said softly at one point. "From the moment I was born and during all the time when I was growing up, they always encouraged me, had me think things through and always set me in the right direction."

On his bedroom wall, Chris has framed a favorite motto that has always been a bible for him for as long as he can remember. It says, simply enough: "obstacles are what you see when you take your eye off the goal." "I like it because it reminds me that dreams can come true for anybody."

And does Chris Burke ever feel that God has treated him unfairly? "No," he said quickly, as though he had heard the question often before. "I actually feel that I have been blessed with God's expectations of me—just to be able to have dreams about doing certain things in life, and then doing them."

And he keeps on doing them. A few years ago, he appeared in another television program called *The Division* and, on another plateau of his bubbling talents, he and his band have recorded their fourth album that combines both inspirational songs and rock 'n' roll. He's also working on still another television production that would be based on his book about himself and his family. It's called, suitably enough, *A Special Kind of Life*.

"I don't want other writers and producers improvising about my life," he said candidly. "So this is going to be my documentary. I'm very strict and firm about that because I want the documentary to be very truthful and very natural." Just like Chris Burke.

It was just about to spill over into noon and Chris had more than a few things lined up for the rest of the day. He started to get up and head for the elevator when I asked him what exactly it is that he tries to get across in his talks before those groups where most of the people in the audience have Down Syndrome. "I tell them just to give it one more shot," Chris Burke said without an ounce of preaching or pollyana. "I tell them to try to make a difference in life by doing different things in their lives. I like to think of myself as someone who is able," he continued. "I feel that I am differently able from other people but still very able to do a lot of things that others can do."

And the lesson that others with Down Syndrome might pick up in the life and busy times of Chris Burke? "Simply to believe in themselves," he said quietly. "To work hard and never give up. Life is not about money. It's really about trying to be an extraordinary person doing extraordinary things. If anything, I would want to be remembered as someone who was involved in a lot of things, especially in entertainment. And I'd like to be remembered as someone who had a wonderful life. That's it. Otherwise, I'm just like anybody else."

And so much more, Chris. So very much more.

ຂχ໑

What is your response to Chris Burke's positive message?

Part II

PAYING
THE PRICE

Guarding the Cross
and the Tomb

FATHER Brian Jordan has always been vintage Brooklyn and the quintessential Franciscan priest in his approach to life, death and people. And that rare combination of street smarts and spiritual instincts was a shining light at the tragic shell of New York's World Trade Center when those twin towers exploded into the sky on that fateful September morning a few years ago.

Although his regular day job finds him counseling a wide array of timid, immigrant strangers to New York at the Franciscan Immigrant Center right next to St. Francis of Assisi Church in downtown Manhattan, much of his time after the horrendous attack was spent at the Ground Zero graveyard of twisted steel, debris, charred human body parts and the acrid smell of death. During all that time, the 48-year-old priest was a familiar figure in his brown Franciscan habit, making his way through the rubble, offering prayers over the bodies whenever they were found and recovered from the wreckage, and offering encouragement, thanks and daily Communion to the rescue workers.

"We can't just talk about it," Father Jordan remarked during one of his more relaxed moments sitting behind his desk while talking about the role of the Church in the months and years ahead. "We have to reach out and be there instead of simply sounding pious about the tragedy and what happened here. What we have experienced here," he said slowly and thoughtfully, "is evil at its worst and goodness at its best."

While he talked, he couldn't say enough good things about the Red Cross and the Salvation Army in those first few weeks after the attack. "I am amazed at the resilience of the rescue workers. They simply never gave up and had a special spiritual determination to find their comrades and the rest of the victims."

Father Jordan then began to talk about the "crosses" that seemed to appear out of nowhere at various points across Ground Zero—huge, haunting crosses that were formed, incredibly, from two large pieces of metal that somehow met and melded together in all the fire and fury of the collapsed buildings.

"I can't explain it," he said, shaking his head. "But some of the workers brought me to this one spot where a huge six-foot cross stood, straight as an arrow. The workers called that spot 'God's house.'"

And as much as he admired all the rescue workers and medical people, Jordan wasn't especially fond of all the politicians who descended on Ground Zero immediately after the nightmare and for weeks afterwards. "They just came to get their pictures taken and then disappeared," he said in disgust. "They all wanted to get their faces in the newspapers and then walked away."

But there were other visitors to Ground Zero in those first few weeks who blamed the whole thing on God. On the very first night of the disaster, for example, some stranger walked up to Father Jordan on the street in a rage and started screaming at him: "Why did God allow this to happen! Why?! Tell me!"

"I tried to talk to him," Father Jordan shrugged, "but he wouldn't listen and walked away. But God can never be used as an excuse for the destruction of something that he created. God created all of us but human beings have the capability to destroy God's gift of freedom. And for every freedom that God gives us, there is an inherent responsibility to honor that freedom. The failure to be responsible for that freedom results in the acts of evil that we have seen here."

Suddenly, the priest looked at the clock on the wall behind him and excused himself. It would soon be time to get down to

"God's house" and all those other mysterious makeshift shrines where jagged steel crosses grow out of nowhere and, even in the face of so much death and destruction, the goodness of man is at its very best as Father Jordan and a few workers kneel down for a moment in all the dust and remember, in soft, unspoken prayer, all that is buried beneath them.

☙❧

Have you wrestled with God's part in the September 11 tragedies?

A Day in the Life of a Special Day

THE drive across downtown Manhattan was hot and clammy and the woman sitting there next to me was cocooned up in one of those ways that, pushing 80 at the time, she was a little girl again. It was still oven-hot when the car eased its way across the street underneath the canyon of windows and fire escapes and old women leaning on pillows at their windows along New York's lower East Side. As we pulled up against the curb where a few kids were splashing each other in yesterday's rain water, a handful of Puerto Rican women were sitting on wooden soda cases outside a bodega trying to fan away the heat.

Dorothy Day, kidding about her big feet, got out of the car and began talking about the chewing gum availability of drugs in the neighborhood. And when I asked why everyone in the neighborhood seemed to own a German shepherd, she simply smiled and pointed to the gaudily painted building in front of us that was her home, The Catholic Worker.

Cane in hand, her black-brown cotton dress sucking in the heat, she moved indestructibly into the house that she and Peter Maurin had opened many years ago and was still as much of a contradiction as it ever was.

The rest of the afternoon was spent sitting and standing and moving around in this clutter of faces and thumb-tacked signs on the walls and simmering onions on the stove, all of it the forever signature of The Catholic Worker in New York. On one wall, there were pictures of Ghandi and Dr. Martin Luther King, Jr. and on another there were strike posters out of the California grape country while a faded old statue of St. Joseph stood over near the window smiling out at the onions and the old woman with the cane.

There has always been the mistake of trying to label this unusual woman and write her off as someone from another time, another place. But sitting there talking with her, a visitor could discover that she loved cold root beer and always carried her rosary beads and was more than a little saddened by the exodus of priests and nuns during the 60s and 70s. And she also carried a picture of Our Lady of Guadalupe in her purse and once searched all over New York for a leper whom she could embrace and, in doing so, find some small trace of humility in herself. The thunder of a plane before take-off always frightened her and she once led the Women's House of Detention in singing Christmas carols during one of her sojourns in jail.

As for her time in jail, she remembered spending thirty days in jail with the Suffragists down in Washington when she was only 18 and another time in Chicago when her efforts with the Industrial Workers of the World landed her behind bars for a mere four days. And during the air raid drills in World War II when she and others refused to take shelter, "it was just a sentence of three days, fifteen days, thirty days. But every time that we were arrested, we did see the inside of prisons where we were finger-printed and searched and it was a very painful experience. I did feel, however, that we could eventually do things to ameliorate some of the conditions in jail from what we saw."

There have always been a couple of issues that Dorothy Day was never very bashful in talking about. One of them is war. Another is holiness. And another is the issue of racism and the Church's record in addressing it. "Racism is still the greatest domestic issue and I don't think that the Church has done a great deal about it. It has constantly sought federal aid for everything instead of using its own resources and its own personnel.They talk about doing all they can but I don't think they do. The churches are locked up all day and there are many places in the churches that can be used for feeding the hungry and clothing the naked. They simply don't want the bother and fuss."

As for holiness, Dorothy Day always ignored the pious jargon of the spiritual textbooks and tried to give it flesh and blood in the lives of the people around her and across the world. "The holy man is a whole man who is more or less balanced and who thinks in terms of the primacy of the spiritual," she remarked, waving to someone who was just arriving . "And I do believe that a great many people are trying to be holy. I think that the young people are trying in their search for spiritual reality even though it sometimes takes them far afield, such as into Zen Buddhism. But if you compare Zen Buddhism to the Fathers of the Desert or the tales of *Sedim,* you get some sense of the oneness of all men in his desire and his hunger for God.

"I don't approve of the actions of the Fathers Berrigan but the fact that they have felt so deeply that they were willing to go ahead and be imprisoned for years for the sake of being mindful of the sufferings of their brothers—isn't that really a wonderful thing? I think these are great changes that are taking place, especially the great emphasis that is being made by people like Dom Helder Camara on working for the poor. I think these are things that are encouraging."

What was not encouraging for Dorothy Day is the suffering, all kinds of it, that so many different people endure. "What saddens me most is the suffering of people," she said softly. "The sufferings of all people. The sufferings of those in authority who sometimes scarcely know what to do and who scarcely even understand what is happening. The sufferings of the poor. The sufferings of all those conscripted to fight in wars. Being stripped of faith, that's the awful part of it. That and the scandal of war."

And somehow in every conversation with this woman, the poor always seem to be its spine and its heart, especially when Christ himself is nudged into the discussion. "We have not been taught very well about him, you know," she said with eloquent simplicity. "But we know where he was and who he spoke with and how he lived. I'm just saying that you should take him literally for the things that he says. Especially about the poor. Remember that every reform in the Church has started with voluntary poverty. Over and over again, with St. Vincent de Paul, for example, and St. Francis of Assisi. St. Francis de Sales too. Voluntary poverty is the basis of all our work."

Dorothy Day was talking about hunger in the streets when it was somewhat politically incorrect. And she was cooking onions and bacon and handing out clothes to the homeless when proper Catholics left that sort of thing to Catholic Charities. And she went to jail for her convictions when Dan Berrigan was still in school.

Catholics sometimes have stunted ideas of just what a saint is so that maybe Harvey Cox's suggestion that people like Dr. Martin Luther King, Jr. and Dorothy Day are indeed the real saints of their time or any time is a suggestion that may leave some people confused and perhaps even slightly miffed. But the mark of the saints has always been their rejection by others, their reputation as fools or renegades, their loneliness in the face of others who never let their charities get in the way of their sleep or their suburban respectability. If some people like their saints plastic and antiseptic, then they should forget about someone like Dorothy Day.

It was, of course, nice to go out and meet someone like this woman while inhaling some of the chipped and boiled-out graces that are all around her. She was actually a very intimidating woman because nothing ever changed her or budged her from doing some of the things that she had grabbed on to with both hands when she was a much younger woman.

The kids were still playing in the rain water and the women were still holding court on their wooden soda cases when I walked out on the street. Dorothy Day stood at the door leaning on her cane for a few moments before waving goodbye. But I had the feeling that she was looking past me down the street where all these others were the beginning and end of everything that had always been so dear to her, everything that was her life.

ↂ

Are Dorothy Day and Martin Luther King, Jr. your idea of saints? Why or why not?

The Man Who Invented Archie

C. O'Connor.

Now at the mere mention of that name, some astute souls might easily surmise that we are talking here about the man in the red robes who, some years ago, presided over all things at St. Patrick's Cathedral in New York with great solemnity and flair.

Wrong. In this particular instance, we are talking about another man who was graced with legendary flair and, when the occasion demanded, almost papal solemnity. Carroll O'Connor grew up in New York, went to school at P.S. 101 in Forest Hills and attended Mass at Our Lady Queen of Martyrs where he remembered that "the pastor was Father Joe McLoughlin and he was boss there for over forty years." You should know from the beginning that there are important, personal reasons for talking about this man, this O'Connor, with the kind of respect and admiration that some people usually reserve for, well, Cardinals.

Of course, there are a few subtle similarities between Cardinal O'Connor and Carroll O'Connor, both of whom left us some years back. They both had unmistakable fondness for the dramatic. They both had excellent connections at the front office. And neither of them was ever above telling anyone they disagreed with to go stifle.

Now while the Cardinal was obviously a decent, if somewhat occasionally irascible sort of chap, Carroll at one time gave me this one great unwashable memento that will never fade away or be forgotten. I am talking here about his gift to the entire world, Archie Bunker, that bumbling, huffing, cranky buffoon who never knew when to back off or give in. I am talking about that paunchy, middle-aged grouch who, once a week, in more ways than one, invariably gave me some of the clearest, crispest insights into who I was in all those carping, critical, cantankerous moments that I have occasionally inflicted on my family, my friends, all of the above.

And that is why I have always felt that I owed Carroll O'Connor, aka Archie Bunker, a special debt. Not that my close-to-a-twin reflection on the television screen cured me any, but at least, once in a while, I had the opportunity to see how ridiculous the Archie Bunker in me looked to the rest of the world. That is why I decided at one time to get in touch with Archie, uh, Carroll and talk with him about some of the things that might be of mutual interest to a couple of old New Yorkers.

At the time, Carroll and his wife, Nancy, and their son, Hugh, lived in Malibu and only occasionally returned to New York to visit his mother, Elise, who still lived in Forest Hills. Earlier, I had visited Elise who still lived in the same corner house where Carroll once lived and where a large framed picture of Carroll, resplendent in his First Holy Communion outfit, smiled out demurely at one and all as they walked into the hallway.

"Thank God she's in such good health," Carroll noted about his mother in that first conversation with him. "And she's as merry and witty today as she was as a little girl. I remember when I was little and she would hold my hand as we went shopping along Fifth Avenue in New York. Whenever we get into New York now, we see my mother at least once a week, usually for Mass on Saturday evening and then dinner afterward."

And did Carroll O'Connor think of himself as an especially religious man?

"Sure. Doesn't everybody? I just hope the Lord thinks I am. As for the Church and some of the changes that have been happening, a full answer would require a book, and I'm not competent enough to write that book.

"But I can say that the changes since Vatican II seem to have made worship warmer and simpler, and easier for people to appreciate. The plain words, 'do this in memory of me' are deeply moving but they were not very moving in Latin, not even understood, even though they are the very message of the Mass. The whole Mass today is more inspiring than it was years ago because it invites us to think of ourselves as participants, real followers of Christ, and not just watchers along the way."

There are, as my family will readily attest, great, cranky gobs of Archie Bunker in many of us. But how much of Archie Bunker actually lurked inside of Carroll O'Connor?

"Something of every character that an actor plays can be found in the actor himself," Carroll explained patiently without once grinding his teeth or rolling his eyes. "When moments of Archie's life had to be angry or loving, I had to make the emotions out of personal substances. As to Archie's prejudices, they were merely an actor's report on the world he has lived in.

"Speaking for myself, I hope that only God may judge my beliefs, and I am glad to leave God to everybody else's beliefs. Generally, I avoid giving judgments where I have no right to judge. Everyone's conscience is between himself and God. Edith was forever trying to explain this to poor Archie in my darling Jean Stapleton's beautifully simple and moving portrayal of a real Christian."

And at this point, I wondered if Carroll could talk for a few minutes about his old neighborhood, some of the old hangouts, where he played ball.

"Ah, Dick, the people who will read this have heard all that stuff before in some of the daily papers. I'd rather talk about some of the things that we've been talking about, religion and the Church."

With that as a cue, I thought about all the times I had sat and listened to Archie complain, from his toes, about the dingbat, about Meathead's appetite, Barney Heffernan's dog and Gloria's taste in Polish deadbeats. Surely, Carroll O'Connor must have some passing complaint or peeve about the Church.

"I don't think I have a peeve," O'Connor replied without even a trace of arched exasperation. "But the hierarchy disappoints me in some ways. For instance, to start at the top, I was dismayed by the pope's ruling that the clergy must get out of politics and devote themselves entirely to the ministry.

"I can't see the conflict in a priest doing both if the spirit moves him. I'm not saying that a priest ought to go into the pulpit and tell me how to vote. But who else will suggest to us how we may examine the issues of the day in light of the Christian ideal? Is the politician to be our only permissible guide to right thinking? If he is, we're in deep trouble.

"The American Catholic bishops' letters have upset a number of politicians and ultra-conservative commentators by very calmly putting a number of bad problems in this country on paper. We have, and have always had, perennial unemployment and miserable poverty in this country. And all the while we have congratulated ourselves on being the world's richest, kindest, most generous society. And that is hypocrisy. And though several social problems still persist, we keep cutting down the people-spending and increasing the war-spending. The bishops' letters examined fiscal problems morally—they looked at the whole issue of the nuclear arms race morally."

Around the time we spoke, someone had made the point in the press that fundamentalist preachers were stealing the thunder from the Catholic Church on television with millions of dollars poured into weekly programs pleading with the faithful to follow their hallelujah trail and, by the way, also make sure to put the check in the mail. So I asked Carroll if he thought the Church was missing the boat.

"Missing the boat?" he repeated, "the boat to where? If our destination is the kingdom of God, I'm not sure the television boat gets us there. I think that religion on television can become a kind of showboat—the star, the spectacle, the exciting words and music. Marshal McLuhan had a thought about just this issue: 'the medium is the message' and that suggests to me that the religious television show can itself become the destination. Being on the boat becomes the important thing, even if the boat goes nowhere!

"I don't know—maybe I'm not considering the question deeply enough. I guess that what we're doing is right, although of course we will always need to be doing more."

And when I asked Carroll O'Connor to describe himself as a kid growing up in New York, his response was immediate and Archie candid. "Innocent. Dumb. Protected by affluent circumstances. On the lazy side. In for a lot of surprises."

And then switching to his life as a celebrity, "lucky, more than I've deserved to be. Wondering when God is going to say, 'alright, now I want a few minutes to chat because I am getting you ready for something.' I am jittery about this.

"There's one last thing. Do me a favor and send along my blessings to all the people who have appreciated my work and given me whatever importance I have as a performer. Also, remember me in your prayers for a special intention. And remember Nancy's mama who has Alzheimer's Disease."

We will never forget Archie Bunker but it's always tough to replace an old neighborhood guy like Carroll O'Connor who, beyond all his success and fame and towering talent, always remained a deeply private, sincerely honest man with dazzling, bare-bones convictions about his faith and the future, passionately immersed in his family, and someone who always had this great, shining gift to make us laugh so easily. And that was perhaps only natural for someone like Carroll O'Connor who could never quite stifle the smile in his soul.

❧

Did any of Carroll O'Connor's responses surprise you?

Death of Another Salesman

THERE was one week, a few years ago, when it was not an especially good week for priests on Long Island. Their ranks thinned down even more when three of them, Father Charles Steiger, Monsignor Daniel Fagan and Father Joseph Lukaszewski died within days of each other in different parishes.

So when, after the last funeral, Father Frank Eisele, told a handful of parishioners at Our Lady of Lourdes Church in West Islip that their 48-year-old pastor, Father Lukaszewski had passed on, he added, simply and sadly, "we're a dying breed" and walked off the altar.

Considering the dwindling number of priests throughout the country and the serious shortage of young candidates applying for the priesthood, Eisele's words may have been all too true. Maybe. Maybe not if numbers are never really a factor.

I will always remember the last time I saw Father Joe Lukaszewski, sitting in a wheelchair in Good Samaritan Hospital, stunned and perplexed after hearing the diagnosis about a brain tumor. I will always remember his homilies, week after week, when he invariably called for ethnic and racial respect for all people and always used the phrase "including myself" when he talked about human frailties and the weakness of man.

I will always remember how he never preached down at people from a high and holy pulpit but preferred instead to talk with them, as one of them, on their own level. I will always remember when, hearing about his death, I thought of Willie Loman and *Death of a Salesman.*

Make no mistake about it. Although he was a different kind of salesman, Father Joe was no Willie Loman. But apart from the tragic life and death of Arthur Miller's classic anti-hero, there is a sharp parallel between most of today's priests and the outline of Loman standing alone in the shadows with his suitcase.

For instance, most of today's priests are, like Loman, hard workers leading a rather lonely and sometimes thankless life, pursuing a dream that will probably outlive them, remaining deeply committed to a parish that is their family, and struggling to exist in a society that perhaps doesn't quite understand them or fully appreciate them.

And just as the world seemed to change overnight for Willie Loman, so in the aftermath of the sex abuse scandal, today's priests have discovered the changing attitudes of people in a hurly-burly, in-your-face society—a more grudging respect, increasing demands on their time and energy from all sides, and little or no security for life after retirement.

Although the maudlin, mushy "priesthood" of Bing Crosby and Barry Fitzgerald died ages ago, thank God, there are still some Catholics who insist that the ideal priest is essentially the statue of candy and syrup that Hollywood always loved to prop up as reality.

That priests are human beings with as many vulnerabilities, frustrations, disappointments, sudden setbacks and failures as the next guy is sheer heresy for many Catholics who never had any real understanding of their priests or the lonely nature of their lives.

But the raw humanity of priests is perhaps their purest link to the rest of us as they go about the routine, and sometimes dangerous business of reaching out to others without falling in. You see, priests aren't supposed to show any weakness or talk about some of the temptations and dead-end pressures that sometimes seep into their day. They're not supposed to get tired and they're certainly not allowed to flaunt their humanity.

Still, a few so-called staunch Catholics get all fluttery and uptight when their priests play jazz instead of Gregorian Chant on their stereo, skip the Roman collar during the week and instead wear jeans and one of the Gap's loudest sports shirts. If Willie Loman had been a priest, he would have caved in after the first scene.

But, as with any profession in any generation, so also in the priesthood there will always be a small percentage of misfits who can't handle a drink or rein in their sexual drives. But unfortunately and unfairly, the faults of a few have scarred the vast majority of priests and jaded the trust of many people who grew up with the belief that their priests exist in some hallowed, impregnable cocoon.

But a few losers are the exception and hardly the rule in the priesthood today or even fifty years ago. For that small few who blow their lives over too many snorts of vodka or secret sex, there are nonetheless other priests like Father Joe Lukaszewski who never strayed from his childhood dream and would kid about his few flimsy warts without being choked by them.

In the end, Willie Loman couldn't cope with his ocean of illusions or handle all the things that flooded in on his job, his family, his life. He felt betrayed and driven because it seemed that life had passed him by and he was being swept aside by everything that was new and young and progressive in every corner of his existence. And that's where the parallel ends.

While a few of the Church's hierarchy occasionally get all lathered up by things obtusely doctrinaire and ethereal, today's priests, with their feet planted firmly on the ground, have simply gone about their work, easing their parishes, and their Church, into the new millennium.

And for all the debate about reinventing the parish or seeing the priesthood evolve into a priesthood of women, married priests and some sort of second-hand, hand-me-down priesthood for the laity, most priests have simply done what Willie Loman could never do. They have embraced today, with all its futility and questions, without wallowing in yesterday or fretting about what tomorrow will bring. They have kept the lives of others in focus as the center of their own lives instead of the other way around—something else that Willie Loman could never do.

A few years ago, three good men died within days of each other while the people who knew them and loved them lost a profound part of their own lives forever. The three of them had lived and died as good and gentle men and nothing nobler could be written across their graves.

In the end, in a terrible time of turmoil for many priests, Father Joe and the others walked off into a peace that is not always there as today's priests try to cope and meet the challenges of a changing priesthood. It is the kind of peace that Willie Loman was searching for all his life.

☙❧

How can you help priests to cope and to meet the challenges of a changing priesthood?

Searching Out the Homeless

THE blue van slowed down as it turned into one of the more desolate corners of the Bronx, a remote loading dock at the Bronx Terminal Market where a few empty trailer trucks were parked. A woman got out of the van and walked over to a huge abandoned warehouse with large, gouged-out holes where there once were doors and windows. Inside, there was nothing but a spooky darkness and, in the middle of a cold and blustery winter day in the basement of the Bronx, its floor was a grimy expanse of rubble, dirt, garbage and worse.

"Annie, are you in there? Are you alright?" the woman called out in the darkness a couple of times before another woman's voice answered faintly from the opposite end of the abandoned cave.

"Over here, Sister. I'm over here."

When Sister Lauria Fitzgerald had worked her way across the debris and filth, she and Annie embraced, the two of them surrounded by the cluttered piles of bags and makeshift bedding that were all of Annie's possessions in the world. And inside Annie, a tiny life was waiting to be born in a few months—her thirteenth child.

As on almost every other day in the week, Sister Lauria had come to visit some of the homeless men and women who were scattered all over the Bronx. They are the major part of her day and they include prostitutes, addicts, alcoholics and others who remain invisible to most of those walking around in the nicer parts of the city. The nun and Annie talked for a few minutes about the pregnancy and about a visit to the clinic together later in the week. Sister Lauria then asked if anyone else was around and Annie pointed to another patch of darkness about twenty feet away.

The nun then found her way over to a tall black man bent over on a cane and obviously in pain. Three nights earlier, someone had stabbed Ray in the thigh and he had lay bleeding in the street until Sister Lauria had come and helped him into the back of her van and over to the warehouse because he had refused to go to the hospital. He had also refused to see a doctor but Sister Lauria , fearful of gangrene setting in, made him promise he would go with her to a doctor when she returned in a few minutes. Ray nodded, fell back on his grimy mattress in the warehouse and later saw the doctor with his friend, the nun.

It was just the beginning of another day for Sister Lauria, a short, puckish, electric Dominican Sister of Blauvelt who, for more than a dozen years, had been driving around one of the more ragged sections of the country while searching out the homeless and helping them in any way possible.

On this particular day, her '90 Plymouth van was loaded with rolls, soda, cheese and muffins when she left the Highbridge Community Center and began her daily routine which usually ends late at night. The back seats in the van had been removed so that she could squeeze more food into it. "I think I bring food to an average of about fifty people a day, mostly at night," she said. "And I sometimes don't get home until about two in the morning. The Life Center gives me about $150 a week to buy food but that can get spread pretty thin. I used to get left-over food from the Bronx House of Detention but that stopped a while ago. But it was a big help while it lasted. As far as getting enough food now, it's a little bit here, a little bit there.

"Besides the food, I try to take some of the homeless to clinics or hospitals when necessary, drive them to visit relatives, go to court with them or else visit them at Rikers Island if they've been arrested. The rest of the time, I'm simply trying to find as many of them as I can and bring them something to eat."

Professed as a religious in 1988, Sister Lauria worked among the poor in Appalachia for seven years before that as a Glenmary volunteer. "I love being with people, seeing where they're at, them accepting me and me accepting them," she said as the van turned the corner and stopped at another abandoned building that had been gutted by a fire. "I've never met such faithful people or people with as much courage as here among the homeless. And as a community on the street, I sometimes feel they have a better community life than some religious communities because they really care about each other."

She then showed off the St. Patrick's Day card that she had received from a woman called Katie. "Katie," she explained, "was homeless for a year and a half and lived over there in that abandoned building just behind Yankee Stadium. She and one of the homeless men got married while she was here and I helped them get an apartment, but the marriage didn't work out. But now, she's living happily in California, has two jobs, attends AA and has been clean for a year and a half. She still stays in touch but I miss seeing her every day with that big smile of hers."

In addition to Katie's card and occasional notes from others, Sister Lauria also has a lot of fake jewelry that some of the prostitutes had given her along with several small wooden crosses that some of the men had carved for her. "I have them all and I will keep them always. I also have a bible that one of the men carved out of a bar of soap while he was in jail. He even carved in a message."

A few blocks away, she stopped the van when she spotted Dennis and Terence. Dennis had lost a few toes to frostbite during the winter and started chatting with Sister Lauria while she put several slices of cheese in a sandwich and gave him an extra muffin. She also talked to Terence about going with him for his Medicare card later in the week. "They live on the street so they don't have an address. So they use my address for all their mail whether it's health cards or social service things or letters from their family.

"The worst times of the years are the winter, naturally, and then the summer," she continued. "That's when all the young gangs are out on the street and they can be very violent and cruel to the homeless. Annie was beaten severely in the park two years ago and one of her eyes still doesn't open. There are a lot of homeless Vietnam vets and I feel so badly about them. They fought so hard and gave so much for their country and here they are out on the street.

"Occasionally, a couple of the men will get into a fight out on the street but I'll keep out of it. When the women fight, I try to break it up but a few times one of them pulled a knife on the other so I backed off. But they are all very protective of me. If someone curses when I happen to be around, the rest of them will get after him or her about their language. And if, for some reason, I don't show up for a couple of days, they worry that someone may have hurt me."

As she drove down a one-way street, there was a loud, cheerful hello from a few of the homeless as they approached the van. They were always glad to see her as she ran to the back of the van to get some food. The only time she didn't smile back was whenever she saw a child.

"As you can see," she said with sudden seriousness, "there are no homeless children around here. It's something that I won't tolerate because there's no reason for a child to be homeless. There are plenty of foster homes and social services has many shelters and other programs for the young. There's no reason in the world for anything else so if I see a child out on the street with the others, I report it without waiting another second."

But for a pregnant woman sitting alone in the darkness of an abandoned warehouse or a man missing a few toes and standing in the middle of the street or a young prostitute wrapping up a favorite necklace for her friend in the van, there is a cheese sandwich and a special pig roast in the summer and the familiar sight of a beat-up old Plymouth weaving its way through the streets.

And there, smiling out from behind the wheel, is Sister Lauria Fitzgerald with her street-smart savvy in a city cauldron, her relentless energy, her loaves and fishes and that pixie smile of hers crackling across the Bronx as the van turns another corner and disappears into the summer afternoon.

❧❧

Who are the Sister Lauria's in your community and what can you do to help them?

Good Priest, Bad Priest

THE second most intriguing thing about the packed meeting room at New York's Queens College was the number of stained glass windows peering down at the group. And one of them, ironically enough, showed a young angel smiling out over the inscription, "suffer the little children to come . . . .."

But the most intriguing thing was the 120 people who had come out on this early Spring afternoon to listen to the author-psychologist and former priest, Eugene Kennedy, talk about the sexual abuse scandal in the Church and the culture of clericalism that was still flexing its muscle. Sitting there in the crowded Newman Center room were priests and former priests from all over New York City, Westchester and Long Island along with a handful of women and a few reporters. They had all come because it was time.

Before the meeting started, one of them greeted a few old friends that he hadn't seen in years while others introduced themselves to an unfamiliar face from Brooklyn or a Roman collar from Hicksville. Most of them were between fifty and seventy years old and, along with one or two former monsignors, there were several pastors but not a bishop in sight. It was indeed an unusually unique gathering of people who had come together for the first time in an upper room at the college, three days before Pentecost.

They had come, of course, to hear Kennedy talk but, as the afternoon moved along, there was the unmistakable feeling there among most of them that something else had drawn them, something else was driving them during the question-and-answer period to stand up and raise their voices and pour out their souls about the sex abuse scandal in the Church that was drowning all of them.

"The most impressive part of the afternoon," later remarked Monsignor Bryan Karvellis, the pastor of Transfiguration Church in Brooklyn and one of the organizers of the meeting, "was the spirit in that room of people who love the Church and love the priesthood. None of them was snarling or negative and it was obvious that each one of them wanted to heal and help the Church. But there was a spirit in that room that you could actually feel."

As it turned out, Kennedy was only incidental to what was happening in that room on that afternoon and to what its mood hinted at for everything in the future. Some of the things that Kennedy said were perhaps thoughts that had already passed through their own minds as the scandal unfolded. Until now, they had been reluctant to air them on their own but now some of those thoughts and convictions and feelings were banging off the walls as Kennedy spoke. And these were not rebels or radicals but stubbornly focused human beings who happened to share a controlled old passion about a Church that they always loved and a priesthood that, active or inactive, in or out, they always cherished.

"There is an unwritten perception among some of the hierarchy that they are the Church," Kennedy said at one point. "But there is a crisis of a hierarchical organization that has collapsed in our time so that we have a vacuum of leadership in the American Church today."

"We want to build on today," remarked Tom McCabe, a resigned Brooklyn priest and one of the organizers of the meeting. "But we also want to speak out on issues, build alliances with other similar groups around the country and invite women and the laity to join us."

And as others stood up to ask a question or make a comment, there were several issues that seemed of great concern to all of them and would be a riveting part of every agenda in the future:

• support all priests everywhere who have been drained and hurt deeply by the scandal;

• reach out to all the victims and their families;

• never forget the plight of the children in all of it;

• invite the media to all future meetings;

• never stop loving one another, including those cardinals and bishops who have faltered. Otherwise, nothing is accomplished;

• address other issues that are troubling and dividing the Church.

"We're not looking to confront or challenge anyone," added Monsignor John Powis. "We're not looking to picket or demonstrate. Our purpose is simply to get people talking about what is happening and to speak out."

"Until now, priests have been the most compliant, and they're the ones who have been most affected by this," later remarked Father James Sullivan, an 83-year-old Brooklyn priest. "Priests have not spoken up but now perhaps, with this group, all that could change and maybe other dioceses will join us."

"As a nurse, I see the scandal as a wound that is being drained," commented Cathy Kelly a former nun, "and the healing could come from this group that truly loves the Church and the face of Jesus."

But the faces of everyone sitting there in that room seemed far more solemn and serious than even the face of that little angel who shared all their concerns and hopes for "the little children" everywhere. It was a day of reckoning for all the aging faces of so many good men sitting there, a day when so many solid human beings, priests and former priests, quietly renewed a few old vows to bring the face of Christ back to the steps of their Church that was suffering still another crucifixion. It was a moment in the history of the Church in New York when some of the very best had come together in a new Pentecost to start back up the mountain and retrieve everything that had been scarred and dirtied by the failures of others.

And it all ended very quietly as the meeting broke up and goodbyes were exchanged as some headed back to their parishes and others to their wives and families as the smile on the angel's face seemed to brighten and broaden.

But one thing was sure. They would be back together again with a few more new faces and someone like Father Donald Cozzens leading the way because, after all, they were only beginning. Suddenly, after all the shock and anger and all too much silence, they had found their voices so that all the old vows, all the old impulses, seemed as young and lustrous as ever.

Pentecost was only three days away but, for all those who had come there together, it had already dawned.

◒✗◓

Do meetings like this give you hope that the Church can be renewed?

Walking the Walk

JUGGLING a telephone and a cigarette, Father Coleman Costello sat at a desk in a small disheveled room that serves as the office for Walk the Walk, this priest's unique answer to a national tragedy that is one of this country's best kept secrets.

Three secretaries were also on the phone in the same office that is cluttered with mostly second-hand equipment and boxes filled with papers and files. But the tall, white-haired 63-year-old priest was oblivious to all of it as he tried to offer a few emergency answers to one of New York's thousands of abused men and women on the other end of the phone.

He was conversing with a 70-year-old woman whose 38-year-old son had recently beaten her and her husband. The old man, who also has cancer, was hospitalized as a result of the vicious beating. Now both are deathly afraid of their son—but they are also worried about what will happen to him if he is arrested.

The phone is only part of Father Costello's day which begins before dawn in his small office on one of the busiest streets in New York's Long Island City. He has met with city and government officials on countless occasions in an attempt to convince them of the severity and frequency of the problem of abuse of the elderly. And he sends a flood of letters to corporate leaders and others in an effort to scrounge up some sorely need funds to keep Walk The Walk going.

The shocking truth about the prevalence of elder abuse is only gradually being revealed. "It is a generally unrecognized and unreported crime," remarked Father Costello when there was a lull on the phone barrage.

"Right now, there are over 50,000 cases of elder abuse in New York City alone, and these are situations that we know about. Who knows how many others have fallen between the cracks?" he explained. "And the number jumps to five million who are being abused throughout the country and these are people who are either neglected or abused physically, sexually, psychologically or financially, and mostly by their own adult children."

According to Costello, the abuser is usually a son or daughter, but sometimes the attacker is a spouse, another relative, a caretaker, a neighbor or even a stranger. And the abuse frequently goes unnoticed because "elderly people are often isolated and stereotyped" and generally the attack takes place "within the four walls of the person's home," the priest added.

Most experts characterize elder abuse as a hidden tragedy that many people can't even imagine and many communities lack both the personnel and resources to deal with it effectively. Only one out of fourteen incidents comes to the attention of the authorities and, unfortunately, many abused old people refuse to report their troubles to the police because they fear reprisals from the abuser, aren't sure the problem will end, or don't want to betray their "loved ones." And a large percentage still feel deeply and personally responsible for the "child" who is hurting them.

According to Father Costello, many elderly people are victimized because of diminished mental or physical health or else because of drug use or stress on the part of their caretakers. And depression is still another factor. "One of the classic signs of depression," the priest pointed out, "is the inability to deal with certain problems." And as a result, many elderly people turn to "self-medication" through drugs or alcohol. And many who live alone suffer from self-neglect because they don't eat properly or take care of their personal needs.

In the seven years since he founded the program, Father Costello has, among other things, broken ground for an innovative new twenty-bed shelter for the abused elderly in the Glendale section of Queens. Although he is a priest of the

Brooklyn Diocese, the shelter will be open to anyone who needs help in New York's five boroughs and in the surrounding suburbs.

Other parts of the blueprint for Walk The Walk—street lingo that, loosely translated, means "practice what you preach"— include counselling services and a drug-alcohol clinic for those elderly who suffer from those addictions. There are also free legal services provided by area law schools and the local bar association. And the program also offers behavior modification counselling for abusers who often have a history of drug or alcohol abuse or some background of mental or emotional instability. The shelter also tracks the well-being of elderly victims for five years after they leave the shelter.

A week earlier, Father Costello had spent most of the mornings on the phone trying to find an agency that would send food to an eighty-year-old black woman who lived alone, had only one leg and was bedridden. Her nephew had been stealing her food stamps and welfare checks for himself and his girlfriend. But finally unable to find any agency or organization that provided emergency food, the priest began his afternoon by carrying a few bags of groceries to the old woman's bedside in Brooklyn.

But even when not personally involved with the victims of abuse, Father Costello tries to raise public awareness about the problem and also let the elderly know where they can turn for help. His message is that there can be an end, hopefully sooner than later, to all the muffled cruelties that continue to happen behind closed doors, and often in the finest of neighborhoods.

For Father Costello, there is also the ongoing problem of trying to raise enough money to provide trained, dedicated staff, adequate facilities and expanded services for those who need help and who are mostly unknown to the public. He has received a few small government grants and has had some local fundraisers as he continues to come, hat in hand, personally seeking out both private and corporate donations.

"People say that I'm tenacious and I guess I am," he laughed. "But I really believe that the system should exist for the people, and not the other way around. It's simple justice."

There was a definite downtime in the life of this unusual priest when he felt some of the twinges of burnout in his work with another outreach project that he had also founded for drug and alcohol addicts. It was around the time that his mother was dying. But it was out of that whole sense of trauma and wonder that his work for the elderly began.

"I remember visiting my mother for thirteen years when she was at the Queen of Peace Residence for the elderly," he recalled. "And all during that time, I had a great appreciation for the problems of the aged and for the sensitivity and love that the Little Sisters of the Poor brought to the people under their care. So I began to study the problems of the aged a little more and discovered that there are so many things that society can do to help them. But we have to be very thoughtful in defining the problems of the elderly so that we can devise the right strategies.

"The most important thing," he explained, "is for all people to accept the fact that the abuse of the elderly exists in every community, that it is widespread, and that too often it is completely hidden." One of his continuing recommendations is that concerned individuals seek proper training in recognizing elder abuse and in utilizing existing resources to address the problem. In addition, he feels that parishes and community groups should offer workshops and develop additional resources to link victims and abusers to the proper social service agencies and health facilities. And bottom line, local businesses and political structures should be nudged hard to support every single outreach effort in their community. Otherwise, the elderly will continue in their shamefully premature fall to their grave.

The phone rang again. And for the next few minutes, Father Costello wasn't really thinking about the small, squeezed office or the loud and cranky traffic out on the street. For those few, fleeting, sacred moments, his only thoughts were on the frail, frightened voice on the other end of the phone.

What can you do if you become aware of an elder abuse situation?

Mother Teresa

"I'M sorry," the secretary apologized, "but they're having lunch now and then Mother Teresa has to get back to the Sisters' convent in the Bronx. I don't think you'll have much time to see her."

The office of Catholic Relief Services on the 13th floor of the new Catholic Center in New York had managed to hold onto some of the bustling veneer from its old office on Fifth Avenue. And now in the middle of this wintry afternoon in 1975, it seemed even more hectic than usual since it was acting as the official host to Mother Teresa of Calcutta during her brief visit to the city on her way to Rome and back, finally, to her work in India.

I had met her only once before, years ago, when she had been in New York on the tail-end of another whirlwind visit for a talk before the Diocesan Council of Catholic Women. I remembered the plain white sari and the sandals and coarse white stockings that she wore then. I remembered her as a very serene, soft-spoken, slightly hunched-over woman who was just beginning to emerge in conversations around the world as a twentieth century saint.

Suddenly, Eileen Egan of the Catholic Relief Services staff appeared in the doorway and announced that Mother Teresa would be able to see me now, but only for a few minutes. I thanked her and walked into a small corner office where this little woman in the familiar white sari, her face tanned and wrinkled, stood up and apologized for the long wait.

I had scribbled a few questions on a piece of paper but as we began talking and one idea drifted into another, I put the paper aside as the conversation went its own way, ignited here and there with an afterthought or an idea that flashed up suddenly out of something that was said, or unsaid.

Born Agnes Bojaxhiu in the town of Skopje in Yugoslavia in 1911, she did not want to talk about her childhood or her early life except to say that it was a very happy time in her life. It was at the age of 18 that she entered the convent of the Sisters of Loreto because of the appeal of their missionary work, especially in India. Her father apparently worked in pharmaceuticals but this was something that she felt was too trivial and unimportant to talk about. She was in full control of the interview.

Whatever tangents the conversation slid into, she stubbornly brought it back to what was the only real issue for her in any of her conversations: Jesus Christ and whatever revolved around him in her own life and in the life of the world around her. Everything else for this woman was superfluous and didn't really matter. It was obvious when she talked about things like women and war and Daniel Berrigan. It was obvious when she responded to my first question without the slightest trace of surprise or feigned humility.

"In the last couple of years," I began, "more and more people in this country and abroad have come to consider you as something of a living saint. Are you embarrassed by that in any way?"

"We're all saints," she said calmly and evenly. "Jesus Christ is living in all of us through sanctifying grace and that, after all, is the essence of sanctity. What else can there be? What else can be added to that? Right now, for me, at this moment, you are Jesus Christ. He is everyone that I meet, wherever I am. We are always, each one if us, in the company of Jesus."

I pressed on. "In the last decade," I said, "it seems there have been more and more people leaving the priesthood and the religious life, especially in this country. And many of those leaving have expressed the idea that their vocation has merely changed, that they are still trying to pursue the same kind of personal fulfillment, the same relationship with Christ and others that they always sought. What are your own thoughts about a changing vocation, and about those who have left?"

"A religious vocation," she started saying, pressing her hands together and leaning forward in her chair, "means belonging to Christ. Our work as religious is only a means to an end, a means to put our love into action. People leaving the priesthood and the religious life are making the means the end, and that's not the real meaning of a vocation. We must love God undividedly. So that when something comes up to divide that love, we naturally fail. Obedience is total surrender and we cannot have a religious life without poverty, chastity and obedience. We cannot serve any master except Christ.

"As for the idea of a changing vocation, no, a vocation cannot change. In the religious life, we choose to be Christ's, to be used by him, to be poor. And that can never change."

"But what about your own vocation," I cut in, not altogether gallantly. "Didn't your vocation change when you left the Sisters of Loreto in 1948 in order to found your own order of the Missionaries of Charity?"

She was already shaking her head in disagreement before the question was even completed and her eyes were very serious and fixed on mine as she began to answer. "I did not change my vocation when I left the Sisters of Loreto to found the Missionaries of Charity. I only changed the dress, the accidentals. It was not a change of vocation. Please make that very clear when you write it down," she said, pointing to the notes in front of me.

And now the questions and ideas came storming out and she didn't seem to mind that those few minutes put aside for me had been long gone as she seemed almost to be enjoying the questions, at least some of them. And when something like the issue of women's liberation popped up, she left no doubt as to her feelings.

"Every woman," she said, very deliberately, "is the heart of the family since no man can ever really love in the same way as a woman. So that by trying to become somebody else, women lose something and, because of that loss, the world is what it is today. My advice to women is simple: stay home. A woman's first responsibility is to be the mother, the heart, the only one who can keep the family together. We are only liberated when we live our life to the fullest as a woman. And that is the greatest liberation of all." She then began to talk about a wide range of issues, and never once looked at the clock.

On poverty in the United States: "There is a deeper poverty here in the United States than in India because it is less known. In India, everybody knows who is poor and who is not poor. But here, nobody knows who is poor or where to find the unwanted and the neglected. In a rich family, a child may be neglected and unwanted and, therefore, very poor indeed. To me, the worst kind of poverty has always been among the unwanted, whoever he is, and wherever he is. In the United States, people see so much in terms of material things that they sometimes can't see the poor or unwanted in their own midst.

"But someday we will all be judged on the premise that Jesus left us: 'I was hungry and you fed me, naked and you clothed me.' All it involves is simply a smile or the recognition that someone is a human being. Sometimes, we will pass a drunk in the streets almost as though he were a non-person. And very often, we may even be the cause of his drinking."

On the old Church and the new Church: "There is no such thing as an old Church and a new Church. It has always been the same Church and only small minds think in those terms. Years from now, others will look back and laugh at our ideas about an old and new Church."

On women in the priesthood: "No woman had a greater reason or better credentials for becoming a priest than Mary. But she chose instead to remain the handmaid. If this was her choice, how can ours be any different?"

On holiness: "Holiness is nothing more than accepting Christ and living his life in us. It means doing his will, whatever he wants. Naturally, we are all tested in one way or another but that's the beautiful thing about God. He lets us choose. Every day, we have to make a choice. Sacrifice, after all, means a life of choosing."

On religion in the modern world: "There is a great hunger in the world today for God. It is obvious in thousands and thousands of people around the world. I am certainly not discouraged by the mood of the world. It is the passion of Christ again in all of us."

On sin: "Today, you don't hear too much about sin. And therefore people don't feel any great need for sacrifice or mortification or even forgiveness for a sin that they never committed. In time, however, all of us will have to accept the reality of sin in our lives."

On the United States: "About your observation that, in one year, the United States spent 88 million dollars on defense, I can only say that anything that destroys life does not come from God. As for Vietnam, again I can only make the same observation. But the people in the United States are very generous and very loving. The problem is that they are surrounded by so many things that they sometimes forget that there are people in the world with nothing."

On herself as a world leader: "I am not a politician and have never thought of being a politician or using my influence. I personally can do nothing. I can only do things that Jesus wants me to do."

On divine providence: "We have never asked for any money for our work and have never sent out a single appeal for funds. We have simply taken Christ at his word that he will provide for us as he does for the lilies of the field. We have never found any reason to be discouraged or to worry about things. The work that we are doing is his work and he will see that it is completed. We do not beg for money from anybody and that is the most beautiful thing of all because it is most touching to see the thoughtfulness of God in even the smallest of matters."

On prayer: "Jesus Christ is the key to my prayers every day. He is in the sacrifice of the Mass in the morning and in the poor during the day. He is whomever I meet. I don't have any special prayers, but I enjoy reading the 15th chapter of St. John. It is very beautiful."

On her weaknesses: "I have plenty of shortcomings, just like anybody else. And when I pray, I pray to be kinder and humbler and I pray for more patience. Yes, I can lose my temper, but not in the extreme. I get angry whenever I see unkindness to those who are feeble."

On the Berrigan brothers: "Before God, both of them felt that they were doing the will of God in breaking the law during the Vietnam war. But they are the only ones who can answer that. We cannot say whether their actions were right or wrong."

On her favorite saint: "I don't have any special patron or any individual saint that I say prayers to. My only interest is Jesus. He alone is the object and center of my prayers."

On her plans for her order in the future: "I don't have any major plans or projects in mind. We simply do our work from day to day, helping the poor wherever we find them."

There was a knock on the door as Eileen Egan excused herself and reminded Mother Teresa that she was already well behind her schedule. Mother Teresa smiled and turned again to shake hands and say goodbye. I had brought along a book that Malcolm Muggeridge had written about her so, as a final request, I asked if she would mind writing a brief message to my children on the title page. She took the book and, sitting down at the desk, wrote out these words: "Make your home another Nazareth where the love of Jesus, his peace and joy binds you and lives in you. God bless you. Mother Teresa." I thanked her again and walked out to the elevator.

A few days later, I called to thank Eileen Egan for arranging the interview. She had known Mother Teresa for more than twenty years and her respect for the woman was as clear as water. "Of all the people I've known in life," she said over the phone, "she is the one person closest to Christ. She sees everything in terms of Jesus. And so do her Sisters. So also does her order of Brothers which she started several years ago as an adjunct to the work of her Sisters. It's that simple." A close friend of Dorothy Day and an acquaintance of Tom Dooley, Egan bristled over the phone at the idea of comparing any of them in either their work or their era.

And at the suggestion that Mother Teresa is a devoutly conservative woman with little or no patience for things like optional celibacy or Women's Liberation, she again showed her annoyance. "Her deeds alone," she said sharply, "are those of a tremendously liberated woman. She simple cuts through all the distinctions about old and new, conservative and liberal, and comes back, as always, to the person of Jesus Christ as she sees him in her daily life. It is the only thing that is important to her."

It was exactly ten years later when I attended an event in New York where Mother Teresa was again center stage at an installation ceremony at St. Patrick's Cathedral for fifteen of her novices. After the ceremony, along with several other reporters, I had the opportunity again to ask her a few tritely tired questions during the press conference. She didn't remember me from a decade ago at the Catholic Center but she listened patiently as I raised my hand and asked a couple of questions. Why do you remain silent while President Reagan spends far too much on arms than on the poor in this country and what is your reaction to Cardinal Ratzinger's criticism of

American nuns for what he calls their "feminist mentality"? And once again, her answers were brief and to the point.

She did not, she began, get "mixed" in politics. Nor does she have the time to get involved with hierarchical opinions about anybody or any group. She looked directly at me as she said that she never asked to be placed on a pedestal but was placed there by the media and feels quite humbly that there is nothing different between what she does and what every American nun is trying to do with their lives. And no, she does not understand liberation theology nor does she believe in a female priesthood but, you asked the questions and those are your answers. What else is there to say? Is there any subject really worth talking about outside of the poor? God bless you and yours.

"Why don't you smile?" Sister Priscilla asked me a day later when I called her convent in the Bronx to inquire about a rumor that Mother Teresa wasn't feeling well. Sister Priscilla, at the time, was the Superior of the Missionaries of Charity in the South Bronx and Mother Teresa's right arm whenever she was visiting America. "I watched you yesterday during the press conference and you weren't smiling," she continued. "And you can do so much to make other people smile."

After I made some lame rejoinder about whatever it is that passes for my smile, Sister Priscilla asked if I would like to come to their convent in the South Bronx and just chat for a while with Mother Teresa—no press conference, no set format before Mother Teresa returned to India in a few days. "There will be no other reporters, no real fuss," she said softly over the phone. "Just you and Mother. I think it is Jesus' hand."

I didn't really feel the hand of Jesus the following Saturday when I drove to the South Bronx convent with my wife who was all excited about meeting the famous lady in the white and blue sari. As requested, we got there at the ungodly hour of seven in the morning, just in time for Mass.

When one of the Sisters escorted us to the small chapel, both Sister Priscilla and Mother Teresa found a couple of chairs for us by the wall in the cramped, perspiring chapel that was crowded with other Sisters, several young women in lay clothes that, we learned later, were considering joining Mother Teresa's Missionaries of Charity and even six young men who were thinking about becoming Brothers of Charity. And everybody, including the five priests concelebrating the Mass, were in their bare feet. It was the first time that I ever had my shoes off in church.

When it came time for Communion, the Sisters and all the others started to file out into the aisles so Pat and I looked at each other and decided that we would wait until everyone else had gone ahead. But just then, Sister Priscilla caught my eye from where she was sitting in the back and nodded for us to go ahead. So as Pat stepped out into the aisle, an old Sister stepped back to let her out. It was Mother Teresa. We had cut off a saint!

After Mass, it was like Sister Priscilla had said, no big fuss. We stood outside the chapel and chatted for a while with Sister Priscilla and Mother Teresa and Pat even showed them photos of our children. "Maybe one of them will join us," Mother Teresa said with a smile as she ran her fingers across the photo of Tricia. She seemed surprised that I knew that she would be 75 in a few days and glowed at the number of young people who had been in the chapel. And as we talked, she was visibly elated about the few hundred houses that they have around the world. She would be leaving in a few days for Paris and, yes, she was feeling fine even though she had a heart condition and a schedule that would test an astronaut.

As we were about to leave, I reminded Mother Teresa of the message that she had written in Malcolm Muggeridge's book ten years ago. "Make your home another Nazareth," she had scribbled. And those words, next to a picture of her holding a child in India, is still hanging in our home.

After Mother Teresa blessed the two of us and said goodbye, Sister Priscilla invited us to come back again soon, even after Mother Teresa had gone, to help her and the other Sisters give out food to the poor in the South Bronx. She was, of course, quite serious and asked us back as casually as I would ask someone to join me for a cup of coffee.

Looking back, it all seemed very right and natural to me on that sweltering summer day years ago when I knelt in a remote Bronx chapel with my shoes off while this little old lady out of India handed me a hymn book as we walked up the aisle. Since then, I have often thought about her, especially after she died, wishing there might have been another time when I could have seen her and she could have pointed out all the right pages, all the right passages.

"Make your home another Nazareth." Could anything be simpler, or more eloquent? And as we walked out the door that day, the last thing on my mind was what this unusual woman thought about Ratzinger or Reagan or the brothers Berrigan. ". . . .where the love of Jesus, his peace and joy binds you and lives in you . . . ."

Pat and I walked out to the car and waved to Sister Priscilla who was standing there laughing as I pointed to my smile. We drove down the street, turned right at the light and headed back to Nazareth.

∞

From what you know of Mother Teresa (now Blessed) and her views, how is she a model for American Catholic women today?

A Priest Forever . . .
and Paralyzed

FATHER James Bradley, sitting in his wheelchair in his seventh-floor office at Catholic Charities, listened attentively to the dumb questions that he had probably answered, with some effort and great patience, hundreds of times in the past.

How did a stroke change your life? What do you say to others who are in the same condition as yourself? Can you empathize with other disabled people who have to fight off depression? Is there such a thing as being disabled without hope?

Bradley, 55, responded patiently as he recalled some of the details of that summer day seventeen years earlier when, without warning or the slightest of symptoms, a blood vessel burst at the base of his brain and he fell to the floor in his rectory room, his entire right side shut down forever at the age of 37.

At one time robustly athletic, Bradley had run in some of the New York marathons and jogged three times a week. He played paddleball with friends in the summer and skied in the winter and now, as his visitor walks into the office, the priest reaches out with his left hand to shake hands

After all these years, he still has his intellect, his will, his sense of humor, but only vague memories of his once muscular body and athletic skills. Now, his right leg is in a metal brace, his right arm is completely useless, and his speech is faltering and somewhat slurred. The muscles in his right eye are damaged and weak and his left eye is partially paralyzed so that he can only move it up and down but not sideways.

And yet. And yet . . . . Disabled but undaunted, Father Bradley is a full-time program specialist with Catholic Charities Office for the Disabled in the Brooklyn Diocese where he spends part of the week visiting pastors and promoting Bishop Thomas Daily's 1992 pastoral letter on the disabled: "Come to Me: The Church's Response to Disabled Persons."

Father Bradley was the principal adviser to Bishop Daily when he wrote the pastoral and, as part of his visits to the pastors, he stresses the need to appoint special parish advocates who will locate and assist disabled parishioners while increasing their own awareness of the disabled and their needs. According to Father Bradley, pastors and priests should become more knowledgeable of the condition, explore ways to improve access to all parish buildings and improve the quality of life generally for their disabled parishioners.

Bradley has also headed the Diocesan Access Commission and has worked closely with the Open Congregation, an ecumenical group that promotes inclusion and accessibility throughout metropolitan New York. And every Sunday without fail, Father Bradley, who is able to stand with some support, goes to the altar to celebrate Mass, preaches a homily and distributes the Eucharist. He has always had a stubborn idea of just what 'disabled' is.

"We could use at least four Jims," said Sister Bernadette Downes, who had been director of pastoral care for the Diocese's Office for Disabled persons and is currently president of the Nursing Sisters of the Sick Poor. "He's very bright, focused in his ministry and can laugh at himself and the rest of the world. He has a great sense of humor."

Bradley's ability to laugh easily is a by-product of hope, forged during those early days when there was so much struggle. "Sure I wanted to know 'why me?' when it first happened," Father Bradley remarked to me that day in his office in 1997. "In the beginning, I was very negative and saw very few positives. But there is no answer. There wasn't then, and there still isn't. God may have a plan, but I wish he would let me in on it," he said with a hint of mischief in his voice.

And after the stroke, did Bradley ever think of packing it all in and leaving the priesthood as something that just didn't turn out the way it was supposed to?

"Oh sure," he said quickly. "It passes through my mind occasionally but I think I can still do good work as a priest. I am touching people's lives and I think I am actually a better priest today because I've learned that, in looking at a person's real value, you don't ask what he or she can or cannot do, but who they are. There is also the simple fact that each one of us is loved by God, and always will be. It was that thought especially that helped me deal with the stroke."

More than most, Father Bradley can readily understand people who, brought down by a severe disability, may be considering ending it all. He is keenly aware of his unusual pulpit and of the eye level that he shares with disabled members of his congregation. "I know that for many of those who are disabled, coming to me, it's not so much what I see but who I am and what they see. I try to remind them not to look at things as obstacles but as challenges that can be overcome, and to look at things not as stumbling blocks but as stepping stones." He also reminds them that life is given, not owned.

"I can understand," he continued, "that at the moment when there is absolutely no hope, there is no point in artificially maintaining (life) support. But otherwise, life is a gift, believe me, and it's something for which we are all stewards, never masters. That's why there can be no rationale whatever for today's 'assisted suicide' because no one ever has the right to end any life. Not ever.

"Disability was always acceptable in our family when I was growing up," he said, adding that he was planning a trip to Ireland the following year with his 64-year-old mentally retarded sister so they could visit County Cavan and County Donegal where their parents were born.

When priests or others complain in his presence about some of their 'crosses', he says he tries to avoid any judgment. "I don't know what they're going through," he said, "just as they don't know what I'm going through. Maybe some of them are more disabled than I am emotionally, but I try not to judge anyone. Each of us has to deal with our own problems in our own way."

It was late morning as Father Bradley wheeled himself over to his computer which the former right-hander handles quite deftly with his left hand. The brace on his leg is more obvious than his Roman collar, a piece of daily clothing that, for this priest, is a brace of another metal.

"I guess my biggest satisfaction is still my pastoral contact with individual people," he said softly. "I enjoy offering Mass very much but I love people and I love working with them. When things are down, I just ask God to show me what his will is for me and how I can do it."

And when people walk into his office for help with their own disabilities and troubles, he invariably reminds them that "you do the best with what you have." Something that this unique man has been doing, quietly and courageously, for more than two decades in what have become the finest moments of his priesthood, the richest moments of his life.

⊘✗⊘

What feelings does Father Jim's story envoke in you?

The Street Smarts of Father Pete

WITH his considerable frame of 6'2" and 320 pounds, Father Pete Colapietro may be one of the more genuinely believable poster boys for vocations to the priesthood this side of Pope John Paul II.

And don't be fooled by the "saloon priest" tag that a few friends who happen to be New York newspaper columnists have mischievously hung on him. He got that strictly because of his days, and nights, as both a bartender and bouncer in a few bars prior to his ordination as a priest in New York. And that label was probably enhanced even more with the revelation that his father once owned a saloon in the Bronx.

But for someone who is a walking vocation advertisement, Father Colapietro's own vocation didn't come all that easily. Entering the seminary as a young man, he stayed with it for a time but then left, disillusioned, during his first year of theology, only a few years from ordination. And for the next three years, he separated himself even more and kept his distance from the Church.

"I was having a lot of fun," he recalled recently as he lit another cigarette in his Holy Cross rectory in the heart of New York's Times Square section where this burly pastor is a very familiar figure in a knock-around neighborhood that still has Damon Runyon written all over it.

"But something was missing so I decided to go back, or at least reapply, because I realized, more than before, that God was telling me 'you don't choose me, I choose you.'" So he reapplied and, shortly after, received a letter from the seminary rector Monsignor Ed Montano.

"I'll never forget one of the lines," Father Pete recalled with a laugh, "where Monsignor Montano let me know, in no uncertain terms, that 'the vote for your return was far from unanimous.'"

Ordained a few years later, Father Colapietro is today the pastor in one of the rowdiest and most rough-and-tumble neighborhoods in the city with a leathery old reputation in the local police precincts for drugs, assault and prostitution. "It's a gem," he proclaimed proudly about his parish. "It's really quiet and peaceful and people are sometimes surprised to find a church in this part of the city. Across the street, about 180,000 people pass in and out of the Port Authority Terminal every day and, in the parish itself, some of the people are quite well-to-do while others don't have enough food to feed themselves." But others, with quite creative skills, make sure that life is never dull at Holy Cross.

"People are always coming to the rectory door with some kind of scam looking for money," shrugged the pastor. "If people need food or clothing, they will get it any time they ask. But we don't hand out money on principle."

If Runyon were alive today, he would have to find a very large niche in his books for this gregariously street-smart, down-to-earth, middle-aged priest who apparently was created to be a priest in Times Square. A close friend of some of the city's top reporters, restaurant owners and celebrities, the hulking priest is as recognizable to most of the natives as the statue of the Fighting Sixty-Ninth's heroic chaplain, Father Duffy, looking out across Times Square.

And a few wags may find humor in Father Pete's freelance ministry as chaplain of the New York City Sanitation Department but the priest is first in line when it comes to poking fun at himself. "The Sanitation Department doesn't deserve me but I deserve them," he once told a *Daily News* reporter. "Just look at the size of me. I have been filling too many garbage pails for too many years."

And does Father ever have those gnawing old doubts that haunted him years ago when he first questioned his calling?

"You always have questions," he said matter-of-factly, "but when the questions come, I always dismiss them as mindless hostility on my part. I really feel that I've always been blessed by God and that he really loves me. And I feel it.

"But I don't feel that I'm unique," he continued. "No matter who you are, you should be aware of people's need for God. And it's there, over and over, in the strangest places—the street, the church itself, the saloons, the subway." And then the conversation sauntered back to vocations and the priesthood.

"If you're going to be a priest today," he said, lighting another cigarette, "you should enjoy yourself in your work and be kind to the people, all of them." And then, so simply and so profoundly, "anyone choosing this life has to be happy with it. He has to be well-rounded and willing to accept any sacrifice, and then enjoy the rewards that go along with that sacrifice. And you have to love God."

The rectory door-bell rang and Father Pete excused himself and went out to answer it and then maybe take a walk around Times Square and say hello to store owners and cops, the hustlers and the homeless, little old ladies and grammar school kids, all of his parish. Monsignor Montano would have been proud.

☙❦❧

What are the attributes that help make Father Pete a good priest?

The (Other) Keys of the Kingdom

WHEN Father Neil Connolly walks into a room, one of the first things that you notice is the large set of keys attached to his belt. It is as if he were some sort of maintenance man, some janitor, instead of the pastor of St. Mary's Church on Manhattan's lower East Side, equipped with all the keys to his kingdom in case a light bulb has to be replaced in one room or one of the doors has to be unlocked for another meeting.

But those keys don't really mean a thing in a parish where many of the parishioners have keys to the rectory and the church and the school hall and wherever else the people come and go as if it were their rectory, their school, their home. And that, of course, is quite natural at St. Mary's where the people have grown to believe that they are indeed the parish, the spine and soul of this lower East Side community of men and women because that is what they have learned to believe, and live, during all the years that Father Connolly has been pastor. But that feeling has been there for years with other pastors and priests who shared their keys with the parishioners as part of a vision of the Church that is just beginning to surface in other parts of the Church.

After his ordination in 1958, Father Connolly spent some time in Puerto Rico studying not only the language but things about the culture that would define his priesthood for years to come. "The late Cardinal Spellman had invited Father Ivan Illich to be something of a mentor for many of us who had been assigned to Puerto Rico," he told me once during a visit to St. Mary's. "And one of his first instructions was that in order to be truly poor like the people we were working with, we had to give up any attachment to our own culture so that we could take on another—the culture of the people we are with. Otherwise, we tend to compare cultures and the temptation is always there to pronounce our own as superior."

101

Illich obviously didn't offer it as a form of imitation but as a way of life. And that thought was never lost on Father Connolly during his first assignment as a priest at St. Athanasius Parish in the South Bronx where he served for seventeen years or at St. Mary's where Cardinal John O'Connor appointed him as pastor in 1985.

Father Connolly no sooner walked in the door at St. Mary's when he was embraced not only by the parishioners but by a sprawling, teeming community that included latinos, Asians, blacks and Jews. Aside from his easy fluency in Spanish and his gut perception of the latino culture, he reached out to both young and old not only as their priest but as someone who was urging each one of them to go ahead on their own, to take the reins, to find their place in the parish, to express their ideas and their complaints and their dreams and perhaps even to run ahead and begin to lead others into an evolving future, an erupting, dynamic Church with the laity in the forefront.

"I have always seen the parish, any parish, as a community of people," the 68-year-old pastor started to explain to a friend once. "And I've realized that the people have different talents and different gifts so that the real role of the pastor and his staff is to promote and develop the gifts of the people so that the whole body of the parish becomes active.

"I'm descended from an age that was both paternalistic and maternalistic and top-heavy with hierarchy and pastors who did all the work and made all the decisions. But today, the lay people have both the right and the calling to do some of that work and make some of those decisions. So that while it is the job of the bishop to elicit the gifts of his priests, it is the priest's job to elicit and animate the people so that they can be ministers in the parish. It is our job to hand over real responsibility to the people so they can exercise real leadership.

"Our vision of the parish has become a reality here at St. Mary's because our entire staff of priests and Sisters is in collaboration with our lay people and we are all essentially equal. Despite the priest shortage in many parts of the country, there will always be a need for priests. But in some ways, we are working ourselves out of a job. Today, the priest's role is essentially to preach and celebrate the Eucharist but all of the other ministries in any parish should be the role of the lay people who are a community of ministers gathered together for the purpose of evangelization. Today's priests are working harder than ever because we are being forced to work for the development of the total Church."

The heart attack that ambushed Father Connolly in 1990 was probably the result of a combination of things, with hard work and long days and nights at the top of the list. He was at a time in his life when others might have considered transferring to some upstate suburban parish near a couple of golf courses and maybe a beach or two. But Neil Connolly wasn't into any of that nor was he into some of the honors and prestige that go with the years and hard work. So that when Cardinal O'Connor announced the elevation of Father Connolly to the lofty rank of Monsignor just before Christmas in 1995, it was not altogether surprising when Father Connolly said thanks, but no thanks, refusing to accept the purple robes and saying simply that the word "Father" was all the honor he had ever wanted.

"I think that the title of Monsignor is divisive within the priesthood," Father Connolly said at the time. "When a few priests are singled out for special honors, it excludes a lot of other priests who have done some great work in their parish or ministry. I don't think there are any objective criteria for choosing one priest over another in giving the title so they should really drop the whole idea. The whole notion of titles is not what the priesthood is about. And it actually sets up a class system within the priesthood.

"I believe in the theology of empowerment," Father Connolly said a few years later. "That's what grace is all about, so that the people can grow along with a parish that has enjoyed their presence, their gifts and their own personal vision of their Church in the world."

It is an unusual place, this obscure little parish on the lower East Side where every nationality and race pass each other every day on the street and often kneel next to each other on Sunday morning. Someone once remarked that there seems to be an unending number of doors throughout the rectory, the church and the school in what is perhaps the purest, mutest symbol of the welcome that is always there for anyone, day or night, coming to the steps of St. Mary's.

So that it is not really unusual to see Father Connolly and some of his staff sitting down and having an impromptu breakfast or lunch meeting with some of the parishioners or to see others drifting in and out with their own set of keys for their church, their school, their home. It is a unique priesthood of immigrant people from the Dominican republic or Puerto Rico or Korea bringing their gifts and sharing their humanity with a bubbling, expressive parish that can rock the church with its latino hymns and that has long since sprinted past an old and beautiful Grand Street vision of what can still be in the entire Church. Father Connolly walked out the door and down the steps with his keys jingling at his side. But there are so many other keys in his life, keys that he has shared with both young and old or anyone else who wants to open the doors into a future that, for anyone at St. Mary's, is already all around them.

Would the kind of shared leadership at St. Mary's work in your parish? Why or why not?

Part III
EVERYDAY SAINTS

When Thanksgiving Is a Turkey

SO what's to be thankful for?

We always seem to be this close to another war, we're in constant fear of terrorists, the economy has taken a nose-dive, taxes are bloated and grammar school kids are being screened at the door for weapons.

Traditionally, Thanksgiving is a lovely day that we set aside once a year to give thanks for all the toys and goodies that we own, all the good, gaudy things that have splashed into our lives and that, please God, won't go away any time soon. It's a day when the turkey and trimmings are the symbol of everything that is nice and juicy in our lives and the football games in the afternoon are part of the dessert. Thanks, God, and keep it coming.

For many Americans, however, the nightmare of September 11th changed forever some of the things in our lives that we always took for granted as part of the red, white and blue landscape—including Thanksgiving. For those who lost a loved one or sat by, week after week, frozen in grief as the funerals of strangers streamed across the television screen, Thanksgiving would never again be a time to count up all the blessings of a surprise bonus, a new cable dish, a big tax refund. It could never again be a day to wallow in all the trinkets and treasures that are, thank you, God, mine, all mine.

From that day forward, most Americans were brought to their knees with the riveting awareness that, for all the parades and platters of food, there have always been only three things in our lives to be truly thankful for: life, love and God. All the rest is just cranberry sauce.

And anyone who has ever walked away unscathed from the smoke and smells of Ground Zero will never again see anything on earth that is more precious than life and love and the breath of God in both of them.

Life, even when it is scarred with sickness and disappointment. Love, even when it is betrayed or lost. And God, even in those dark moments when He seems aloof or asleep as so many thought He was on that fateful September morning.

It is impossible to imagine one without the other or to define one of them without including all three. They are the only true trinity that has always defined the real meaning of any thanksgiving and are far more personal and enduring than all the plastic games and cool Armani clothes that spell happiness for so many of us. What else could we possibly be thankful for? Our American Express card? Toys R Us? The Sopranos?

So we embrace life and are thankful that we were created by God, warts and all, with all the potential to eventually become the people we were meant to become from the beginning of time. And, rich or poor, we can always be grateful for those shimmering moments in our lives when we have loved another and, pure bonus, have been loved in return. And since the artist in God etched out His two great masterpieces in life and love, there can be no valid thanksgiving for anything in creation without His name in any of it.

Spiritual writer Henri Nouwen noted that "true spiritual gratitude embraces all of our past, the good as well as the bad, the joyful as well as the sorrowful. From the place where we stand, everything that took place took us to this place, and we want to remember all of it as part of God's guidance."

But perhaps no one more eloquently expresses the poignancy of life, love and God in any of our lives than the young single woman on Long Island who cares for her seven siblings, all of whom have Down Syndrome, while she herself valiantly faces every day with an inoperable brain tumor. "I have a strong faith and I believe that God will take care of me," 32-year-old Kathleen Lutz said to a reporter once. "I'm here for a reason. I'm here for them and they're here for me."

So no sermons, please, when Thanksgiving comes around again this year for Kathleen Lutz and her young family on the gut meaning of life, love and the presence of God in their lives. They are the sermon. They are the epitome of everything that even transcends Thanksgiving and whispers about other, sometimes painful things that eventually touch all of us.

It will perhaps be all too easy for some of us as we count all our blessings on Thanksgiving, look piously to the heavens and wonder what the poor people are doing. The sufferings of others are sometimes the impetus for all our expressions of thanks when they are actually the awkwardly fearful feelings of relief that we are not among the homeless, the bedridden or those wolfing down a bowl of soup from a prison cell. Thank you, God. Thank you very much.

But suffering and loneliness, as Nouwen notes, are all part of the package and nobody has ever gotten a free pass when it comes down to sickness, heartache or loss in any of its tortured faces. Still, there are many of those, beaten down by tragedy, despair and the rock-bottom shadows of failure who have taken all the suffering and setbacks that have come along, put them in their pocket and used them to dig out strengths within themselves that they somehow manage to cling to in moments of pain. They are discovering a resilience at the pit of their troubles, a resurrection and a will in some of their darkest moments that complete them as human beings in the ultimate thanksgiving of their lives. It is why so many who have so little to be thankful for are far more grateful on Thanksgiving than some of the rich who save their thanks for their reflection in the mirror.

In that moment, when we can accept some of the heartache and loss that come along as part of the deal of being human and embrace them as the fabric and fulfillment of life itself, it is God Himself who gives thanks for the shared life and love that we bring to the table for others and, blessed or broken, reflect out across every day of our lives.

What are you thankful for today?

Now Pitching for the Poor . . .

MY memory has trouble with what happened yesterday. I lose track.

And yet, I will never forget that balmy early autumn afternoon, more than fifty years ago, when the Dodgers' Ralph Branca threw a pitch and Bobby Thomson hit it into the left field stands in the old Polo Grounds for the pennant-winning home run in 1951 and Giant fans everywhere, myself included, entered into the kingdom of heaven.

Since that day when I remember sitting in our Manhattan kitchen listening to the game on the radio, there has been Muhammad Ali, Michael Jordan, Tiger Woods and other fabled legends of a golden era in sports. But for me, there will never be anything quite like those few fleeting seconds when Bobby Thomson leaned out over the plate and sent Branca's second pitch soaring out over Andy Pafko's head in left field and into the lower deck. I can still hear the announcer, Russ Hodges, howling hysterically into the microphone: "the Giants win the pennant, the Giants win the pennant, the Giants win the pennant . . . ."And I can still see Leo Durocher and Eddie Stanky rolling around in the dirt along third base in a wild fit of delirium. I can still remember The Miracle of Coogan's Bluff.

There may never be another game like it but it's nice to know that Ralph Branca, despite the shattering loss, went on with his life and did things that paled anything that others, Thomson included, might have done with a bat and ball. With the help of a few other ex-major league ballplayers, Ralph Branca started to do something for former players, down on their luck, that should get a special shrine, all by itself, in the baseball Hall of Fame in Cooperstown.

"I first became interested in B.A.T. (Baseball Alumni Team) shortly after I left baseball," Branca recalled recently at his home in Mount Vernon, New York. "Over the years, B.A.T. has helped countless people, both men and women, who were once associated with baseball in some way but, along the way, ran into some tough times.

"In that time," he explained, "a lot of us have been able to help guys who played in the old black leagues, guys from Latin America, even some of the people who worked in baseball offices, umpires and the widows of ballplayers who have passed away."

Branca went on to say that while the names of all those who have been helped have been kept anonymous, there are a few former ballplayers who have publicly thanked B.A.T. and the people associated with it for what they've done for them and their families. For the former Brooklyn Dodger, Sandy Amoros, it was an artificial leg. For the family of Denny McLain, the ex-Tiger pitcher, it was paying the bills while McLain was in jail for gambling. For Blue Moon Odom of the Oakland A's, it was shelling out the rent money while Odom was climbing back out of the bottle.

Branca also made a point of emphasizing th fact that while the baseball Commissioner's office picked up the tab for all extra expenses, the Equitable Life Assurance Society contributed $780,000 to B.A.T. over one period of time. He also singled out some of his colleagues in B.A.T., former ballplayers like Joe Garagiola, Warren Spahn, Larry Doby, Bob Gibson, Frank Torre, Rusty Staub and sportswriter Bill Slocum as the driving forces behind B.A.T.'s efforts and success in reaching out to those who no longer heard the roar of the crowd and could no longer feel the rush of adrenaline walking up to the plate or out to the pitcher's mound.

Today, while hundreds of major league ballplayers earn multi-million dollar salaries and millions more in promotions, Branca, who won an incredible 75 games before he was 25, never earned more than $17,500 a year in his best year. Unfair? By today's standards, sure. Unjust? Of course. But again, people like Branca never measured success or life itself in dollars and cents but rather in values and interests that are all but obsolete in today's big-bucks sports. For someone like Branca, there were other perks.

"There was always a good feeling about helping people who once played ball but later ran into some bad luck," Branca said a few years ago to a friend. "Life's been very good to me and my family but I'm glad that I've had the chance to help a few people who didn't get all the breaks. And besides, they brought back an awful lot of good memories about people who've been good friends for years in baseball."

And there will always be memories for Ralph Branca. If you ask him, he will single out Eddie Stanky, Clyde King and Gil Hodges as his closest friends when they all played for the old Dodgers back in Brooklyn. And he still remembers getting married in St. Francis of Assisi Church in Flatbush and immediately putting his initials on the legend and legacy of the Dodgers as he stood on the pitcher's mound in Ebbets Field during all those fairy tale summers when the world was a little boy sitting in the sun with an old beat-up baseball glove.

"Let's face it," Branca suddenly said with that warm, easygoing, we've-been-friends-all-our-life smile of his. "Baseball is just a microcosm of society and baseball players face the same kind of problems and tragedies that others face all the time." And let's face it. Branca and his pals with B.A.T. were one of the brighter sides of baseball when they put their lives on hold while they reached out to those in their fraternity who had fallen on bad times. In all that time, they've been a warm and welcome throwback to that time in all our lives when heroes did indeed walk the land and called themselves Dodgers and Giants—and even Yankees.

Like I said, my memory has trouble with what happened just yesterday. And as the years slip by, even the glorious memory of Bobby Thomson bounding around the bases has faded slightly and slipped into the crevices. And yet, I think I will find it hard to forget this other man who was once the enemy on the hated Dodgers, this gentle, soft-spoken man called Ralph Branca because it will be hard to forget how he and his friends have brought something to baseball that is so very decent and refreshing and lustrous.

Standing taller in so many ways than many who have played the game, Branca has had the kind of stunning performance in his life after baseball that is all too rare in most sports today. With the kind of quiet dignity and grace that have always been there for this man, on and off the field, he has done more things with his two arms and his game-day heart than most people, in or out of baseball, ever dream of doing.

The Miracle of Coogan's Bluff is gone, done, over. But there have been all these other miracles that Branca and his friends have sent soaring into the sky with the kind of quiet generosity and concern that are as bright and warm and beautiful as any afternoon sun that ever splashed across old Ebbets Field when he stood out there on the mound and somehow stood taller than even he can remember.

๏ปฟ

There are many Ralph Brancas who personify the "pay it forward" theme. Whose story can you add to this Hall of Fame?

The Heat and Hate, Under the Sun

THE four men, all Mexican, sat in the living room and talked quietly about what it was like to be an undocumented day laborer living in a suburban Long Island town at the beginning of a new century while trying to support their families back in Mexico.

Of course, there were twelve other Mexican men, three women and a young boy living there in the same house. But crowded living conditions are the least of their problems as they go out every morning looking for work that most Americans would consider an insult, a demeaning slap in the face. But if there is grass to be cut, houses to be painted or strong backs needed to carry out junk, they will stand in bunches on street corners waiting for strangers to drive by and hire them for the day at a minimum wage.

On the wall above where they were sitting on a battered old couch, there was a small, six-inch cross made of palm branches. And above the doorway to the living room was a plastic bust of the Holy Family. And over on the mantelpiece near the window, there was a faded old picture of the Sacred Heart alongside a statue of Our Lady of Guadalupe.

Otherwise, the rooms were mostly Spartan bare with very little furniture, lighting or fresh paint. And in the tiny kitchen near the front door, someone was frying tortillas next to a big bowl of soup.

"None of them had a very easy time coming to the states," explained Marist brother Joe Madsen, a tall, burly man who works with the Brookhaven Spanish Apostolate and served as a translator for the visitor. For each of the men there, the trip into the United States from Mexico was something they will never forget—a long, grueling, often dangerous journey across the desert from Hidalgo, Mexico and, if they were lucky, into Arizona.

Gregory, 34, explained that he had spent 25 days alone in the desert and Alberto, 21, said that sometimes there were days when there was no food or water. Roman, 46, admitted that there were more than a few moments when he wanted to turn around and go back to Mexico. And Brother Joe said that he had heard stories from others of finding dead bodies along the way. There were still other stories of men drinking their own urine in order to survive.

But perhaps that was the easy part for these mostly young men and women who, like the Irish and Italians and countless others before them, came in search of the "gold in the streets" and the holy grail of security and a happily-ever-after paradise in the states. But the cold, fish-eyed glare of racism has been a mean constant in their lives ever since they opened the door to the U.S. Immigration Office in Arizona and later walked the suburban streets of Long Island's Farmingville in search of work, even a whiff of acceptance and a friendly face. But there was one moment a few years before when welcome for two young men was a ride to a deserted patch of land on the outskirts of town with a couple of young rednecks who proceeded to beat them to the threshold of death.

"There have been times when I've actually been called a traitor to my country," Brother Joe said softly while talking about members of a local civic group (most of them Catholic) who virulently opposed the presence of a single Mexican in their community or the interference of anyone who tries to help them.

One of the groups, facetiously called the Sachem Quality of Life Organization, was successful in pressuring the local politicians into shutting down a hiring hall for the Mexican workers in one town and vetoing a bill to build a hall that would have been conducted by Catholic Charities.

Yet, on any morning of the week, small groups of young Mexican men can be seen standing on street corners waiting for landscaping or construction trucks to drive by and offer them jobs where they could sometimes earn $80 to $100 a day.

They can also be seen in restaurants washing dishes or working as bus boys, or in nursing homes where their job is to clean up after patients who lack bowel or bladder control. "The Catholic Church has been the only refuge we've found here," remarked Gregory, wearing a tattered old baseball cap. "They are the only ones we could trust, the only ones who tried to help us and encourage us."

"But many white people have been kind," added Alberto. "When we first came here, there was no place to live and we had no money. And some of the people treated us as if we had no dignity. But in all that, the Church was the one place where we found welcome and help." But that reaction was always missing in a small handful of Catholics who didn't want to see them kneeling next to them in church.

"I have been called the enemy," remarked Father John Derasmo, the pastor of Resurrection Church in Farmingville, "There is one group that claims I am aiding and abetting illegal aliens who, 'by their presence here, are breaking the law of the land.' Some of them even urged our parishioners to hold back their contributions to the parish. Fortunately, our parishioners ignored them."

But according to Father Derasmo, the large majority of people in Farmingville are not racist or intolerant "even though many have expressed their concerns", added the priest. "Some people have raised the issues of health problems and crime fears but the Mexicans have caused no problems in either area, and they don't seek charity. They simply want to work so they can help their families in Mexico."

Others, he said, fear a decrease in their property values, a loss of local jobs because of the Mexican workers and the crowded housing conditions because of the presence of more than a thousand undocumented Mexicans.

"As a pastor, my concerns are for everybody in the community," Father Derasmo continued. "I've tried to find a common ground but these opposition groups don't want to hear anything except the deportation of all these men and women back to Mexico. Anti-immigrant groups try to discredit the Catholic Church but we have to address the needs of these day laborers in the light of the gospel. This is who we are as a Church and the pope has repeatedly emphasized our preferential option for the poor."

"The two largest groups of 'illegal aliens' currently in this country are the Irish and Polish," smiled Brother Joe Madsen while sitting in the rectory of Our Lady of Mount Carmel Church before driving out to the rented home of one of the workers. "But nobody notices them or complains."

"Some day I hope to go back to my family in Mexico," chimed in Roman who, along with many of the others, has been on Long Island for more than three years. "I send back everything that I earn because they need it so much at home. But maybe some day I will be with them again."

For these young Mexican men and women, however, that dream seems far away at the moment, and the road ahead a little longer and lonelier and perhaps even more treacherous than that walk, a few years back, across a boiling desert.

ᘒᔓ

Would the kind of shared leadership at St. Mary's work in your parish? Why or why not?

Marching to a Distant Drum

IT being that time of the year when it is one of the planet's great high holy days for anyone even pretending to be Irish, St. Patrick's Day is always a cue for the Irish to have that little extra snap in their swagger. The amateurs, of course, will wear loud green ties and silly plastic hats but most of the Irish will dutifully fulfill all of the truly spiritual obligations of the day by going on their annual pilgrimage to Fifth Avenue in New York and watching the parade, fervently and religiously, as if it were High Mass itself.

There have been times, of course, over the years when I wanted to skip the parade because people always seemed to sneer at the parade as a one-day carnival and the only authentic signature of the Irish in New York. As if all we had to offer were the bagpipes and banners of the Counties sailing up the street along with a few shameless politicians prancing along, pathetically, for the sake of a few extra Irish votes and their picture in the paper. As if the boozing of some of the teenagers on the sidewalk and the blather of the television announcers were some sort of March 17th tradition in New York and not a hell of a lot more.

But, excuse me, the Irish have always had so much more to offer whether it's St. Patrick's Day or the 4th of July or Super Bowl Sunday. And it's not just the music or the fabled, feisty history or the legions of poets and dreamers and heroine housewives who have touched every culture and every country. It's been a lot of different people, in the arts and business and even politics, marching to their own distant drums. And it's been someone like William J. Flynn.

If Flynn, once upon a time, had never left Cathedral College and his studies for the priesthood, who knows what the lad might have been. Bishop? Archbishop? At least the president of Fordham?

But neither the Catholic Church, most of Ireland, nor his pretty wife, Peggy, and their four children will ever hold it against him that, years ago, Bill Flynn chose to follow another road, a different drummer. If you scan through the pages of his life, William Flynn has chaired more boards of directors, assisted more charities, and been honored by more institutions and civic and religious organizations than most statesmen and certainly than most of the so-called movers and shakers growing old and stale with their afternoon tea.

Add to that the fact that, as chairman of the board of Mutual of America Life Insurance Company and the person primarily responsible for its lofty position in corporate America, he heads up one of the largest and most successfully prestigious insurance companies in the world.

And at an age when most men are refining their golf swing or counting the days until retirement, Flynn took over the presidency of the Knights of Malta in the late '90s and proceeded to put his own strong imprint on this ancient order of Catholic men and women that stretched across the globe. Not only did he streamline the organizational end of this sometimes stuffy group with a tight chain of command but he also made sure that the Knights' charitable and missionary efforts reached even deeper into the cracks and crevices of the poor around the world. In the few years that he served as president before handing the reins over to someone else, he brought the Knights of Malta into the 21st century and onto a plateau it had rarely managed to climb in its long history.

But perhaps the clearest insights into the mold and mettle of Bill Flynn sparkled through in the late '90s when a couple of stoic Irishmen visited him in his Park Avenue office, talked about the troubled battlefield in northern Ireland and then suggested, as only Irishmen could, that if Flynn really wanted to help, he should put his money where his mouth was.

And Flynn, taken back a little, proceeded to do just that. In all the years that have followed, Bill Flynn has traveled back and forth between New York, northern Ireland and London while serving as advocate, arbitrator, counselor and international broker as he tried to bring all sides to the table in order to hammer out a peaceful solution to some of the centuries-old pain and punishment in his family's homeland.

On countless occasions, he has hosted meetings at his New York office where people like Gerry Adams, Martin McGuinness and Irish Secretary of State Mo Mowlan, all major players in the drama of northern Ireland, came and aired their views before returning to Ireland with Flynn to continue the talks that eventually brought all sides to at least the promise of a lasting peace.

Those two Irishmen who had come to his office with their nervy dare had indeed touched something in Flynn's psyche when it comes to a challenge. Irish to the bone, Flynn probably knew all along that it was the kind of challenge that had been there when he started mapping out something as outrageous as his own insurance company or when he took over the reins of the Knights of Malta or when he said yes to countless administrators and bishops who came knocking on his door asking him to help them raise money for this or that cause that was suddenly Bill Flynn's cause.

With the energy of a few Marine platoons and the zest of a little boy for whatever he happens to be doing at any given time, the thought of retirement for Bill Flynn, even in his early '70s, probably won't cross his mind until another few decades have come and gone. A deeply devout Catholic, a giant in corporate America, and probably the most loyal friend anyone could know, Bill Flynn has always been as comfortably at ease at a business board meeting or a conference of bishops as he is in the company of a few old neighborhood guys or the next stranger to come out of the crowd and shake his hand.

It was only a few years ago when the Irish marched up Fifth Avenue on their high holy day and, as the music brayed and the crowds cheered, the man leading the whole shebang up the street as Grand Marshal was, of course, himself, Bill Flynn. In their own way that day, the Irish were telling the world that, there in front of it all, was the embodiment of everything in the Irish that is good and generous and ready, by all that is holy before God, to take on the world. They were leaning over to tell their children and grandchildren that there, right in front of them, people like Bill Flynn, in so many towering, lustrous ways, are the parade.

∽⤬∾

Retirement for those like Bill Flynn just means a continuation of hard work in the service of others. Tell us about them.

Faith, Hope and Maybe
a Home Run

FOR any baseball fan sitting just behind the New York Mets dugout on a balmy Spring afternoon at Shea Stadium, the scene unfolding out on the field was sheer utopia.

As some of the players and coaches tossed a few baseballs around or stood at home plate in the batting cage before the game, one of them would occasionally trot over to the dugout and playfully lob a few baseballs into the crowd of kids leaning over the dugout roof and yelling for a baseball, an autograph, anything that they could take home and point to, with great pride, for the rest of their natural lives. It was a scene, up close and personal, that Little Leaguers dream about and that older, diehard fans would always recall, a close encounter with one of their gods.

And there in a corner of the dugout, getting his catching equipment together an hour before the game with the Arizona Diamondbacks, was the Met catcher, Mike Piazza. A few weeks earlier, religion had become the focus of attention, and some controversy, in sports circles when a few ballplayers brought God into the clubhouse with special chapel meetings, born-again conversions, post-game prayers on the sidelines and clashes with management about the unspoken separation between God and the games.

Charlie Ward, a basketball player for the New York Knicks who frequently wore caps or T-shirts with the word "Jesus" on them, had defended the right to conduct prayer meetings in the clubhouse and even quoted the Bible about historic attacks by Jews against Jesus and Christianity. And the sports pages of some of the New York newspapers were suddenly sounding like stuff in the diocesan press.

And when someone strolled into the dugout and asked Mike Piazza about the issue, he leaned back against the wall and looked out at the other ballplayers having a catch or taking their cuts in the batting cage. "Actually, I think it's a good thing if some ballplayers are discovering, or rediscovering, their faith," he said matter-of-factly. "I was born Catholic with two very devout parents so naturally I was brought up that way, with their beliefs and their faith.

"I'm very proud to be a Catholic," he continued, "but, for the most part, Catholic athletes aren't as vocal or demonstrative as others are on the issue. I love being Catholic but I don't try to force my beliefs on others in a way that would probably turn them off."

At 34, Piazza could probably be an effective spokesman for the Catholic Church but his style, low-key and laid-back, is geared more to what he does than to what he says. He doesn't wear his religion on his sleeve but, when asked about it, he will gladly talk about it with a mix of quiet enthusiasm and humility that is unusual for someone who steps into the limelight every day.

"Part of the problem," the future Hall-of-Famer explained, "is that people often think it's hypocrisy when they see certain players pushing their faith publicly but then making mistakes with something else in their lives. Maybe some of the players are lost and are simply searching for something, and religion gives them a way to feel good about themselves. For me, part of being a Catholic is that we accept the fact that we have faults but, with God's help, we can move on."

That afternoon, Mike Piazza would strike out three times against the Diamondbacks but he would brush it off as just part of the game, having hit five home runs the week before. His reaction to the strikeouts would also reflect what he had said earlier while sitting in the dugout.

"I have faults like everybody else so I don't claim to be perfect," he said casually. "That's part of being human. We live life the way Jesus would want us to live but we often fall short, as everybody does. That's why society has to work on the presence of religion, faith and family in all our lives because their absence has caused too many of today's social problems."

Earlier in the day, since it was Sunday, Piazza had attended Mass in the same stadium chapel where he attends Mass every Sunday when the Mets are home. It is something that didn't end when he signed a multi-million dollar contract and became a New York icon. It is something that he never lost or traded in for a big dose of celebrity.

"My mom always said that it's easy to forget Jesus when things are going well," the catcher said while putting his pads and mask in a pile beside him. "So we shouldn't only pray to Him when things are going bad and we need Him. We should be there for Him all the time, as He is for us. I've always thought of Christ as the Good Shepherd, a very patient and loving teacher who is always there for us, in hard times and even in the good times.

"I believe that my whole life has been blessed by God, from start to finish, with a good family, good health and a talent in baseball," he added, standing up and getting ready to take his turn in the batting cage. "When I hit a home run, I don't think it's because God willed it one way or the other. God gave me a certain talent, but I also work hard at using it. And that's the image I would want kids to see in Mike Piazza. Believe, very firmly, that you can't take God out of what you're doing in life, and that you always have to give Him 100%."

When his playing days are over, Mike Piazza hopes to do some broadcasting and raise a family of his own. Meanwhile, while others, in and out of sports, miss the point about religion and relate it simply to church and ritual and Sunday, someone like Piazza tries to give his faith as much as it has given him and, in doing that, he doesn't preach or wear it on his uniform or even wear a Jesus cap. But it is there whenever you happen to be talking to him about it and all of it is as real and riveting and vintage Piazza as his next home run.

☙❧

Why is Piazza's "laid back" religion effective?

The Man Behind
Hagar the Horrible

"TO look at Hagar the Horrible is to see Dik," a friend of Dik Browne once said of the man who created the popular comic strip, "Hagar the Horrible."

You've met Hagar, of course. He's that shambling, shaggy Viking who grunts out daily from about 1,400 newspapers worldwide. He's the bumbling, bulbous-nosed barbarian who plunders and pillages the countryside, eats like a starving army, guzzles down anything that pours out of a jug and is pretty much of a lazy, chauvinistic slob and grumpy, forlorn breadwinner. But according to newspaper polls, husbands and fathers have universally taken Hagar to their hearts while many wives and mothers recognize an all too familiar face hiding behind those whiskers.

And when he was alive, Dik Browne saw more of himself in the disheveled Hagar with his scraggly beard and battered shield than he did in Hi of "Hi and Lois," another of Browne's creations and popular comic strips. Browne started collaborating with fellow cartoonist, Mort Walker, on Hi and Lois in 1953 and then began Hagar as his own project in 1973. Much more polished (and bathed) than old Hagar, Hi and Lois are a couple of harried young suburban parents in the frenetic mold of Blondie and Dagwood.

"It has been said that the younger Dik Browne somewhat resembled Hi," Browne once remarked, "but with the onset of maturity, cholesterol, fatty tissues and a wild beard, I've grown to look more like Hagar." And his family agreed. His son, Chris, once referred to his father as "a teddy bear—mainly Hagar, with some essence of Hi."

Mort Walker used to laugh about Browne's dressing habits, his total disregard for color coordination or "even matching socks and shoes." Walker mentioned one particular day when

Dik's wife, Joan, noticed an especially jarring clash of colors and couldn't resist cracking, "I hope you get lost because I'd love to describe you to the police."

Walker also talked about the time when a would-be mugger stalked off in disgust because Browne had so much junk in his pockets, the mugger couldn't find the money!

There was never anything shambling, however, about the number of awards that Dik Browne received during a distinguished life that ended just a few years ago. He was the only cartoonist in the world who ever received the Reuben (the Oscar of the comic art world) for two different comic strips. He also won four Best Humor Strip of the Year Awards, the Elzie Segar Award (named after the creator of Popeye) and the prestigious Silver Lady Award which is given by the Banshees, a New York club of communications executives.

But Browne's genius around a drawing board produced more than cartoons. During a brief fling at advertising after his discharge from the Army in 1946, Brown originated the Birdseye bird, redesigned the Campbell Soup Kids and created the famous Chiquita Banana. And typically modest about all of his success, Browne often said that he regretted never following up on his childhood ambition to become a newspaper reporter, despite all his accomplishments at the drawing board. "I would have liked to have been Willie Scoop," he laughed.

Introduced by a friend to Bishop Fulton J. Sheen on one occasion, Brown did some volunteer cartoon work for him and illustrated seven of the bishop's books including *Life Is Worth Living.* And for Sheen's television show of the same name, Browne was the behind-the-scenes blackboard "angel" who illustrated the bishop's messages through playfully insightful drawings. And right up to his death, Browne attributed his very successful career to his wife, his family and "the grace of God."

All his life, Dik Browne loved talking about Joan Marie-Theresa Hosey Hegarty Kelly Browne, the woman he married sometime around 1940. "The first time I saw her was at the Newspaper Guild while I was having lunch with two other guys. She walked in with a couple of other ladies and sat at another table. And I remember leaning over and telling one of my friends that I was going to marry her some day. Well, I managed to meet her and, a year later, we were married. Joan is the chief source of my success, such as it is."

And about one of the other sources of his success, "Unlike many Vikings, Hagar never carries away maidens. This is the result of a heart-to-heart talk with my daughter, Sally, who is Chinese and adopted, and who saw this as a criminal act and an affront to all women. My two sons, on the other hand, have cooled my naturally bloodthirsty nature so that you never see Hagar actually hurting anybody, although he obviously doesn't obtain his loot as the result of a simple request."

Dik and his other son, Chris, had a habit of carrying around small notebooks so they could capture some of the hilarious things that they saw happening to the Hagars and Hi and Lois's of this world. And clan Browne never missed a deadline since they prepared the comic strip six weeks ahead of time and the Sunday strips ten weeks ahead. But family life was the day-to-day parchment on which Dik Browne and his sons sketched out the eat-drink-and-be-lamebrained adventures of Hagar and the highly amusing bringing-up-father escapades of Hi and Lois. The Browne household was always a close and happy one and it showed in the way that their ideas about family and home and children fell together on paper so humorously and so warmly.

"I'm an addicted family man," Dik once told me when I noted that family seemed to be central to both of his highly successful strips, even in those moments when Hagar is leaving hearth and home to invade the hinterlands. "It's no accident," Dik explained at the time, "that most of the great comic strips have been about families, be they hillbilly (L'il Abner), immigrant (Jiggs and Maggie) or middle America (Blondie). Hagar is simply a Dark Ages version of the same theme—family. You have to understand that Hagar is Everyman trapped in a world he didn't make and surviving the best that he can with the best of motives. Instead of catching the 8:05 commuter train, he hops aboard the 8:05 longboat."

For Dik Browne, laughter was always a lifelong vocation. "The most important thing is to be funny," he once said. "All I want is a giggle a day, that's all—just to have Hagar and Hi and Lois and the others make someone want to smile. The most important part of my work," he said with impish glee, "is when I receive a letter from a woman who lives 25 miles from the Arctic Circle in Norway and she tells me, 'Hagar is just like my husband!' "

The origins of Dik Browne's vocation as a cartoonist go all the way back to his earliest days attending parochial school on New York's East Side where he was born. "At St. Ignatius School," he recalled, "I broke the hearts of the Sisters of Charity. Despite their best efforts, I failed every course, but they did allow me to draw on the blackboard.

"I remember drawing a Christmas mural in the first grade. But unfortunately, my drawing continued right through arithmetic papers, spelling papers and everything else until Sister Everesta, trying to save me, warned 'if you don't stop drawing all those funny pictures, you're going to end up in the hot place.' She was an amazing prophetess because, sixty years later, I'm still drawing those same funny pictures and it's a remarkably hot day here in Sarasota."

When he lived in Sarasota, Browne and his family attended St. Thomas More Church. And when I asked him once if he thought Christ had a sense of humor, he immediately remarked "oh, I would think that he did. But let's face it. His writers weren't exactly writing the Jackie Gleason Show. That's why I have never thought of Matthew, Mark, Luke and John as rivals of the Marx brothers, but 'good news' is happiness and happiness beats humor. I think that humor is God's aspirin for man."

But religion and moral themes have often creeped into Dik Browne's work. And there were two strips in particular that he recalled. "In one of the strips," he remembered, "Hagar and his son, Hamlet, are looking across at the mountains when Hamlet suddenly asks, 'who made the mountains, Dad?' And Hagar answers, 'God.' There is a pause and then Hamlet says simply, 'he does nice work, doesn't he?'

"In the first panel of the other strip," Browne continued, "when his trusty warboat is being washed up on the rocks in the middle of a hellacious storm, Hagar looks up to the heavens and yells out, 'why me?' And in the next panel, a voice from heaven shoots right back through the rain and lightning, 'why not?' "

In his last few years, there wasn't a whole lot in Dik Browne's life that would make anyone want to laugh, especially someone who loved life as much as he did and who loved his family even more. He suffered from cataracts, glaucoma and a detached retina but he always kidded about it and deftly deflected any sign of concern from the outside or self-pity from inside. "It has made me draw a bolder line," he said, laughing. "Now maybe I can draw funnier people." The words and mood and smile were always upbeat and cheerful. Always thoroughly Dik Browne.

My first contact with this rather humble, unpretentious man occurred in 1968 when, out of the blue and a complete stranger to Browne, I wrote and asked if he would illustrate a poster that could be used to recruit foster parents for Angel Guardian Home in Brooklyn where I worked at the time. A few days later, a beautiful illustration came in the mail depicting Hi reading bedtime stories to his children sitting on his lap while a few likeably ferocious "snap-dragons" and "dandy-lions" growled their way across the top of the poster in the children's imaginations. There was no bill or invoice—just a handwritten note expressing the hope that the poster would help find a few foster parents for some homeless children.

And today the world is a much better place because Hagar the Horrible, with his beady eyes and pathetic little sword, still has continents to conquer and meals to slobber over while Hi and Lois continue to bring a twitter to every parent who has ever carried out the garbage or watched helplessly while their children ran up the phone bill. And it is a much better place because Dik Browne always saw things in life that were at once funny and warm, hilarious and human, and, for all that he brought into the lives of millions, even holy.

Matthew, Mark, Luke and John would have been proud. Serious guys, they weren't as funny but somehow Dik Browne's vision of life and love and family was right out of the gospel.

ري‍

Isn't it a bit much to think of life as portrayed in cartoons as being holy?

For the Child About to Die . . .
There's Big Marty

"IF you keep fighting, we'll keep fighting," Marty Lyons whispered into the darkness of a hospital room several years ago.

No, it wasn't one of those brisk autumn afternoons when Lyons starred as an All-pro defensive tackle for the New York Jets in the National Football League, pleading with the offense to score more points. Nor was it even a few years earlier when he was an All-American on fabled coach Bear Bryant's national champion 1978 Alabama team, trying, as Lyons always did, to inspire the entire team.

When Marty Lyons said those words some years ago, they were uttered in the darkness of a Long Island recovery room where a young boy named Peter, motionless and breathing through a respirator, was fighting for his life. That day, Lyons stayed in the room with the youngster for a long time, sitting with the boy's parents. And just before leaving, as Lyons leaned down and whispered those words, Peter's hand suddenly reached out and groped for Lyons' hand.

"It may have been one of the greatest satisfactions in my life," the 6'5" former professional football player said to a friend afterwards. "Years later, Peter is still alive, and still fighting."

But that experience is really nothing new for this giant of a man who has been visiting children at their hospital bedside for almost two decades. It has become part of his life. In another sense, it has become his life. And while it is never really easy and often emotionally draining, he keeps coming back to all these children and to all those moments when a little boy or girl reaches out for the soft, strong hand of help and hope that belongs to Marty Lyons.

For anyone who ever watched Lyons play tough, smash-mouth football during his twelve years with the Jets, it may be hard to imagine this gentler, more vulnerable side of the man. As a football player, he was a punishing, bruising tackler who took no prisoners and was the ringleader of a notorious defensive unit that was nationally known as "the sack exchange."

"When I crossed the line on a football field, I wasn't very spiritual," he said without smiling. But the spiritual world of Marty Lyons swerved sharply in the Spring of 1982 when, within a period of just seven days in March, his first son was born, his father died and a six-year-old boy, for whom Lyons had been a Big Brother for three years, died of leukemia.

"It all happened so suddenly and so quickly, between March 4th and March 10th, especially with the loss of two people who were so very special to me," Lyons recalled. "At the time, I just asked, 'why? How could God let this happen?' I was stunned and questioned my faith as a Catholic."

But the birth of his son provided an answer as Lyons found some measure of peace, and reason, in this new life, this fresh young reason to believe again, and perhaps more deeply than ever before. "I suddenly realized the importance of life," the brawny athlete reflected as a few photos of his family peeked out from a corner of his office. "I realized also that this was God's way of telling me that there's more to life than football."

And so it was that the Marty Lyons Foundation was created after he called a few friends and, together, they began to build an organization that would be totally dedicated to helping children with terminal illnesses and children who have been diagnosed with chronic life-threatening diseases. Since that time, more than twenty years ago, the Foundation has reached out and helped thousands of children ranging in age from three to seventeen, and the numbers keep growing. And in all that time, Lyons and the others visit the children in hospitals, talk to the doctors and nurses, and are a constant presence to the children, lifting their spirits and the hopes of their families.

"We simply try to fill some special wish of all the children," Lyons explained, "whether it's meeting a celebrity, going to a baseball game or Disney World, or doing anything else that they want and that comes within the guidelines of the Foundation."

"And it's not just a one-shot deal," added Martin Kiffel, one of the founders of the Foundation. "We stay in touch with all the children to see how they're doing and we also meet with the parents, doctors, nurses and social workers. These are very special children to all of us."

"Unfortunately, many people in society are too often intimidated by these children," Lyons went on, leaning back in his chair. "They turn to someplace else with their time and concern because the prospect of doing anything for these children seems too much for them. That's why it's so important that even young people understand the problem and what we're trying to do. I think that today a sense of personal commitment is something that has been lost in too many corners of society. And that includes a commitment to our own family, to our children's education, and to religion itself."

In its first ten years, the Marty Lyons Foundation raised an average of $200,000 a year and Lyons proudly points out that, in any year, 95% of the money goes directly to the children while the rest is spent on incidentals such as informational brochures and stationery. "All of our people volunteer their time in the various Foundation chapters in New York and New Jersey," the athlete-businessman-advocate explained. "Then we also have those who contribute money and other resources in fulfilling the kids' special wishes. And there are also dozens of athletes and celebrities who are as close to the children and the mission of the Foundation as they could possibly be." And here he singled out former Jet quarterback Boomer Esiason, former New York Islander Bobby Nystrom and former Jet coach Rich Kotite.

"But there are a lot of other people who like what we're doing and would like to help us if only they had the time," he continued. "But they can always help in some other way. I just ask them to give us their thoughts and their prayers."

"He's a big teddy bear," Martin Kiffel once said while describing Lyons to a visitor. "Kids love him and their parents are attracted to him as someone who is simply a good, generous person. It's not unusual to see him carry a couple of kids in both arms during our annual Christmas party. And it's just the way he is. It's something that the kids just sense, and so do their parents."

There are other interests and causes that take a few more hours out of Marty Lyons' ordinary day outside of the Foundation and his family. Over the years, there have also been the Boy Scouts, the Special Olympics, the Leukemia Society and his time as an analyst in the television booth during the football season. But at the end of most days, there are those moments alone when Marty Lyons remembers that touching moment in his life when a little boy reached out to him in a way that hundreds of others still do, in different ways, at different times.

"If you keep fighting, we'll keep fighting," they each hear him say, over and over, with his soft, husky whisper. So they keep fighting, and living, and fighting again another day. And so does Marty Lyons, every day, for every one of them.

∾⌒∾

In addition to your prayers, is there some organization that you have chosen to share your time and talent with?

Part IV

Surprises Along the Way

When the Admiral Came to Town

THE Coney Island Texas Lunch Diner across the street was suddenly a friendly cup of coffee as I stepped off the Trailways bus that had just lumbered into Scranton, Pennsylvania. It was eleven in the morning on a gray, sullen day and I was slightly early for my interview that would help me write a six-part series for the *New York Post* introducing the new man on the block to all of New York.

I still have my notes from that first trip to Scranton in 1984. I still have a few faded memories of the two-and-a-half hour bus ride from New York's Port Authority and then that first handshake with Bishop John O'Connor of Scranton who had just been appointed archbishop of New York by Pope John Paul II. I still have the feeling that it was only yesterday when I sat down with the archbishop and, over the course of two separate visits, chatted with him about everything from guitar Masses to his days as a Navy chaplain (he retired as a Vice Admiral) to his battles every night with insomnia. I even asked if he ever had any childhood sweethearts and, quicker than the wind, he laughed that he "had left them crying on every corner."

A week earlier, Steve Cuozzo, one of the editors at the *Post*, had asked me to interview the new archbishop for the series that would conclude on St. Patrick's Day, two days before O'Connor's installation at St. Patrick's Cathedral. The series, replete with photos of O'Connor from his childhood to his years on the briny seas, would, Cuozzo hoped mightily, blow away the *Daily News* and *The New York Times.*

Inside the Scranton chancery, I expected O'Connor to be archbishop-pompous, especially for a guy descending on New York from the boondocks, from thirty years at sea as a chaplain and from the kind of clerical obscurity that was one of the reason why most Catholics, and a lot of priests, never even heard of O'Connor.

But in those first few moments sitting alone with him in his first-floor office, there was nothing posed or pompous about him. He spoke with his legs crossed and recrossed. He talked slowly and reflectively in a way that, at times, became a little rambling. And there were the first few unmistakable flashes of a sly sense of humor.

As it turned out, I was the first reporter to interview the new archbishop but certainly not the last. As I sat there with him, he had no objection to my tape recorder while I jotted down a few scribbled notes as he began talking about his appointment. Small plastic red rose in his lapel that I would later learn symbolized his strong pro-life convictions. Simple cuff links. Long, thin fingers. A painting of a schooner on the wall behind him. A neat, Spartan-clean desk. Very friendly. A quick wit and a blue-collar laugh. And a little surprised when I ended the interview abruptly and headed for the door because I had to catch a bus. The buses out of Scranton ran every four hours and I didn't want to spend the next few hours in the Coney Island Texas Lunch Diner looking out the window.

A week later, I had my second interview with the new archbishop and when it concluded, I thanked him for all the time he had given me, shook hands and wished him well in New York. Throughout all the time that we had talked across both visits, he never once ducked any questions, never once brushed me off with a frosty no-comment (as is the custom in a few other chanceries that will go unnamed), never once tried to change the subject.

Instead, as he talked and I listened, the tape recorder inhaled everything that he was recalling with slow, stream-of-consciousness exactness about his brother and two sisters, his book on Vietnam which, looking back, he would have revised, his cement-hard views on abortion and his abbreviated stay in Scranton. And I kept scribbling. Dick Tracy nose. Doesn't smoke. Hair neatly combed in pompadour style, but not exactly Elvis.

As I started to leave, his press secretary, Mary Ellen Keating, called after me and handed me a small cardboard box containing "a gift from the archbishop." It was a square, marble paperweight with his coat-of-arms and his Episcopal motto as archbishop of New York: "There can be no love without justice."

Looking back, thanks to the new archbishop's candor during those two interviews, I was able to predict a few things about the man in that 1984 *Post* series. "Let the word go forth," I wrote in one article, "that he will tolerate no middle ground regarding the absolute authority of the pope." And again, "there will be occasions when his style and delivery will hardly be nice and homey and pleasant. When the subject is abortion or the pope's pique over some rebellious faction in the American Catholic Church, then count on the sermons of Archbishop John J. O'Connor to be anything but mild and mellow. These two subjects will wave a bright red flag for him in the pulpit." Plus a few other issues that always made headlines when he spoke.

On the few occasions when I would meet him again over the years, he always called me Riccardo and was as warm and friendly as he had been in Scranton during those first few visits. In his first few weeks in New York, *The New York Times*, the *Daily News* and the *New York Post* invited him to luncheon with their editorial staffs and, to my surprise, he accepted the *Post's* invitation over all the others because he obviously liked the six-part series in the *Post* and even mentioned it at the luncheon. There were other times, later on, when he might have retracted and ate out at McDonalds.

But apparently, he had no objection to my prediction that a strong anti-abortion stance would be one of his primary crusades while in New York, that he wouldn't be very bashful about expressing his opinion on just about anything, and that he would see the media as a useful tool, as long as they didn't criticize him. In the years that followed, New York would learn, firsthand, about his pro-life passion, his sometimes volatile opinions and his ongoing love-hate relationship with the media.

"Reporters don't set me off at all," he had joked with me in Scranton. "I enjoy reporters. My low boiling-point is political manipulation of the abortion issue. I sincerely believe—and this is not a party-line or a parroting of the pope—but I honestly believe that unless we can stop abortion, we are a doomed society because we are going to end up just destroying our young. We're going to destroy our old, our crippled, our retarded, our cancer-ridden—there will be no end."

Over the years, there were other times when, like a mouse squeaking up at a lion, I was critical of Cardinal O'Connor for being too much of a "sheriff" in the Church, for his lack of shyness around purely political issues and for hosting a meeting at the New York chancery office with far-right zealots like Jerry Falwell and Pat Robertson. Looking back, I should also have thanked him for some of the quietly thoughtful things that he did for me.

For instance, on the day that he was celebrating his first hundred days as archbishop of New York, he graciously agreed to still another exclusive interview about his reflections on the occasion. So while I sat next to the driver and he sat in the back of the car with his press secretary (and now bishop) Monsignor Edwin O'Brien, we talked about a wide range of issues while being chauffeured to Westchester for Mass with a group of cloistered nuns. Among those subjects were his sharp differences with Governor Cuomo on the issue of abortion and columnist Jimmy Breslin's criticism of O'Connor for being more obsessed with abortion than with the poor in Central America. We also touched on education in the city and his public dispute with Mayor Ed Koch about discrimination against homosexuals.

"I feel a grave responsibility for the oppressed in Central America," he remarked, responding to Breslin's column. "But for anyone to belittle my concern for the unborn in favor of the poor and oppressed there, as though you could only be concerned for one cause at a time, is a little childish."

And his greatest satisfaction after his first hundred days in New York?

"It was that one night about a week ago when I got six hours of sleep," laughed the chronic insomniac who rarely averaged more than four hours of sleep during all his time in New York.

The day the interview appeared in the *Post*, Governor Cuomo personally called me on the phone at my office. "It's someone who says he's Governor Cuomo," my secretary, Betty, said, trying to hide a snicker. "It's probably one of your crazy friends." But it was Mario himself and he immediately, and angrily, demanded that I retract as untrue my comments in the *Post* that he and the new archbishop were obviously at odds on the issue of abortion. It was Cuomo's testy contention that he and O'Connor couldn't be in more agreement on the subject. Uh huh. I never retracted a word and Cuomo never called again. But their years together in New York were historic testimony to their positions on the issue, and the distance between them.

But perhaps the most memorable recollection of the archbishop came during one of those interviews in Scranton when I casually mentioned that my brother, Jim, was about to undergo serious surgery for throat cancer. A few days later, Jim received a letter at St. Vincent's Hospital from the archbishop: "Dear Jim, your brother visited me here in Scranton and told me about your surgery. I want you to know that you have been very much in my prayers and will continue to be. My warmest hopes for your rapid recovery. You are in my Masses as well. Faithfully in Christ, John J. O'Connor."

I didn't really say enough about John J. O'Connor in that *Post* series over twenty years ago or in some of the columns and stories that followed. Nobody ever did. He was always outspoken and blunt on any number of issues and said things and went places that might have been forbidden territory to his predecessors, Cardinal Terence Cooke and Cardinal Francis Spellman because of holy prudence and hierarchical discretion. But O'Connor brought a rough-and-tumble style and a no-nonsense, in-your-face defiance of politicians and fools. And he was always deeply, deeply warm and compassionate to the poor and the outcast, to the working stiffs in the unions and to anyone else who walked into his life off the street as he was, long, long ago, to the reporter, Riccardo.

But maybe I came close to another prediction and a more personal portrait of the man when I wrote about his letter to my brother in one of the last paragraphs of that first *Post* story. "It was a small, obscure act in a large and sometimes cynical city by a man who is about to write something else that will be very genuine and very beautiful in our streets and in our history. The name is O'Connor and the address is New York. And if you're looking for him, he's the one sitting down in the middle of a busy day to send his prayers, his love and his 'warmest hopes' to someone he has never even met."

It's probably too late now but my apologies for that 'sheriff' stuff, your Eminence. But my thanks, always, for so much more.

ᘓᕽᕽᗡ

What impresses you the most about Cardinal O'Connor?

The Roof Over Covenant House

NOT many corporate honchos have the same numbing schedule that Sister Mary Rose McGeady had before she retired as president of Covenant House in the summer of 2003. This cheerfully unflappable woman had been the boss ever since Father Bruce Ritter was forced out under a cloud in 1989. Since then she had been the roof and strong foundation of this internationally renowned residence for troubled youngsters. Since then, she had been its heart and soul.

A Daughter of Charity with the street smarts of any of the 150 teenagers at Covenant House in midtown Manhattan, 75-year-old Sister Mary Rose directed a worldwide operation that would boggle the mind of most business executives. With 61,000 youngsters under care in 2003 in Covenant House in the United States, Canada, Nicaragua, Mexico, Honduras, Guatemala and Costa Rica, she had an annual budget of $118 million, 92% of which she received in donations while the other $8 million came from the American government to assist in her care of homeless teenagers.

And barring the advent of any faith-based initiatives, she received no other federal funds and nothing from New York City, the State or the Catholic Church so that it was almost a stark necessity to send out over 750,000 appeal letters to the public every month. The cupboard was almost bare right after Father Ritter was ousted amid accusations of alleged sexual misconduct and the donations to Covenant House dropped by almost 30%.

"But gradually, a lot of good people saw what we were trying to do and came back to us with contributions to our work," Sister Mary Rose recalled at her desk a few years ago. "In 2001, there was a 1% drop because of the economic slowdown in the country. It doesn't sound like much but a million dollars went a long way in our day-to-day work.

"But even in bad times, I always told my staff never to turn away any youngster who came to us for help," she added. "It's a policy that we always had and that will never end at Covenant House."

Besides the 11-story building in midtown Manhattan, Covenant House also has a center several blocks away for pregnant girls and teenage mothers with infants as well as a crisis center nearby. There is also a day care center in the main building as well as seven other community offices located in some of the rougher parts of the city where, as Sister Mary Rose says, "we always tried to head kids off at the pass and, with the help of the schools, identify those kids who were on the edge." In the year 2000, Covenant House received more than 58,000 crisis calls from youngsters all across the country.

"The biggest crisis that we face in this country today is the deterioration of the family," she added. "Most of the kids who come to Covenant House are from broken homes or single parent families. Many of them have been passed around from grandmothers to aunts to cousins all their lives, with no permanency and no stability. And while most of them are poor, a lot of middle-class children run away and come to Covenant House because their father is drinking or their mother is on drugs."

A native of a small Pennsylvania town, Sister Mary Rose feels that the foster care system in this country is in real trouble because, most of the time, the foster parents are rarely home together due to outside commitments in jobs for each of them. And this can be especially critical for children who need special care.

"The biggest tragedy of all in foster care is that most of those kids are discharged to themselves at 18 with no money, no job, no home and no family," she reflected, shaking her head. "And that's when many of them travel a long way and knock on the door at Covenant House."

With more pride than poetry in her voice, she noted that most of her charges were city kids who "liked the excitement of living at Covenant House and getting a job here. And none of them were sent by the police, the courts or the churches. They came because they were homeless and, at 18 and 19, they had no place else to go."

And that is one of the reasons for the job-training program through which the young men and women at Covenant House learn special skills—from construction to computers—for life after Covenant House. Those who eventually find jobs keep a third of their salary, give another third to Covenant House for rent and put the final third into the bank, Sister Mary Rose explained.

"Then when they are ready to leave, Covenant House gives them back all the money that they had given as rent," she added. "There are about 800 companies out there that call us when they have entry-level jobs available and it's a great opportunity for our kids." She then went on to point out that the average stay at Covenant House is a year and a half and at the crisis center it's usually 28 days. "Covenant House has only four rules when youngsters come here: no drugs, no alcohol, no weapons and no fighting. It's really a small miracle that we've rarely had any trouble while I've been here," she said.

And if someone were to ask, religion plays a large role at Covenant House, "as much as it can be encouraged," she noted. She also noted that a Franciscan priest, a Sister of St. Joseph and a Protestant minister serve as pastoral ministers, counselling the teenagers and also meeting them in small groups. "There is also a 'prayer and share' session that usually draws about twenty kids every night when they stand in a circle and say individual prayers that would sometimes break your heart."

"I've heard kids say, 'let my father stop drinking' or 'when I call my mother, please don't let her hang up,' or 'I'm so scared, please let me find a safe place to live after I leave here.'"

But Covenant House is still that safe place in all their lives and, while she was there, Sister Mary Rose McGeady was the roof that sheltered and the rock that supported every youngster who came there to find hope, love, security and, eventually, themselves.

"There was never any greater satisfaction for me," she said softly, "than seeing a kid who was once so down-and-out and depressed, now smiling and confident when he walked out to his job in the city. You can't beat that. But Covenant House has always been about opportunity for these kids. And that's clearly the work of the gospel."

∾⨯∾

Despite the black mark left by Bruce Ritter, why is Covenant House still worth supporting?

The Queen of the Soaps

SCENE ONE: (Agnes Nixon smiles that great, blue-eyed smile of hers as she opens the door, says hello to her visitor, and then hangs his coat in the hallway closet. Her 12th floor Manhattan apartment is elegantly furnished without being pretentious or preening and the photos and assorted knickknacks are a warming hint that family and friends and memories are more important to this woman than crystal vases and snobbish oil paintings. She offers her visitor a cup of coffee which he declines and she then leads him into the living room where he sits by a window and opens his notebook while Agnes Nixon sits on the couch. Action. Camera.)

Ryan: (Leaning forward in the obligatory pose of the reporter) Does it bother you that you have been referred to as the queen of the soap operas?

Nixon: (smiling) Not at all. Everyone gets a nickname in life at some time or another and I suppose that's just one of mine.

Ryan: (Looking at his notes and trying not to be distracted by the notion that Agnes Nixon, soft-spoken and pretty, closely resembles Alice Faye, his childhood flame from the movies that he still remembers smiling out at him from the big screen while dancing away with old John Payne.) Is it true that almost ten million people watch *All My Children* every day?

Nixon: Yes, it is. We've been very successful and much of that is because it's an ensemble effort and the result of the actors, directors and producer working hard together in an atmosphere where every program is regarded as opening night.

(Camera fades to left as Ryan is painfully aware that his rumpled suit and unshined shoes do not exactly blend in with the general ambience. Cut.)

If anyone ever sits down and writes a script about Agnes Nixon, there will probably be parts of it that will sound very much like a routinely dramatic re-write of one of the many soap operas that she has created and written. But there are other parts that would be the classic biography of one of those unusual women whose life far outdistances the glories of her gaudiest heroines.

It may be that Agnes Nixon is one of the best kept secrets in show business, and in the Catholic Church. But she has never really gone out of her way to shine a spotlight on her prolific talents in television while far lesser show biz talents jump up and down for a few lines in the gossip columns or the chance to sit down with Jay Leno and talk about their poodles.

Only recently widowed, Agnes Nixon has been as much a pioneer in television as she has been a creator, writer, packager and producer of some of the most popular daytime soap operas on daytime television. After creating her first series, *Search for Tomorrow,* she then gave audiences *One Life to Live* and co-created *As the World Turns.* After that, she served as head writer for *Guiding Light* and *Another World.* Just warming up, she then created *Loving* and *All My Children* (the MY refers to God) and began introducing to daytime television such socially relevant themes as child abuse, the Vietnam war, AIDS and several other gut issues that other, more timid writers and producers wouldn't touch.

"I try to be as honest as I can," remarked this tirelessly energetic woman who got her first job writing radio dialogue three days after graduating from Northwestern University. Today, she still commutes back and forth between her Manhattan apartment and her home in Rosemont, Pennsylvania. And the visits with her four children and all her grandchildren are pure bonus.

"I think I've been very successful in showing life as it is from day to day," she added. "I've always felt a strong sense of personal responsibility because of the huge audience that watches us every day. It's a very humbling feeling to realize that so many people are watching."

As sophisticated as she is razor-sharp about the swings and swoops of modern culture, Agnes has crafted scripts that have lit up the lives of millions of viewers for decades. And as a writer who happens to be Catholic, she is especially unusual in that she is quite deeply religious without wearing it on her sleeve or inventing some token nun for half the scenes. And yet, her convictions and life ethic are always in there somewhere between the lines, always hidden in there somewhere with all the soap.

"I've been shaped by religion in everything that I do," observed the woman whose life has been a guiding light of sorts as her world turns every day. Her parents split up when she was only a few months old and she was then raised as an only child by her mother and grandmother. With not a lot of playmates, and no brothers and sisters, she used to cut out paper dolls from the comic strips and, little by little, began to create the magical world of Agnes Nixon.

"We have a mandate to entertain people on television, but I also think that we should look at every issue and be able to talk about it. We can't be ostriches," she continued, "putting our heads in the sand while others have to face these same problems every day of their lives."

And then while her visitor in the rumpled suit sat there and scribbled down the words, Agnes Nixon said something very softly that maybe dramatized the only real plot that has been the central theme of her life as a Catholic. "Religion, pure and simple," she said quietly, "is feeding the hungry, clothing the naked and taking care of the orphan. There is really nothing that is more important than simple charity."

As the rumpled suit looked up, Agnes Nixon's eyes were glistening with something that confirmed that she is a very unique, deeply sensitive woman who, in a world of make-believe and cutthroat show business, has some granite beliefs and values and cares very deeply about those beliefs and the people, even the ones she doesn't even know, who are part of them.

If there was indeed the slightest film of emotion as she talked about religion and the way she sees it in the faces of both friends and strangers, it was hardly the stuff of soap operas. It was the soft, sincere signature of Agnes Nixon on another day about the things in her life—from her family to her work to her religion—that she has always cared about quite deeply without any fanfare or spotlights.

And none of it is rehearsed or scripted as her search for tomorrow ended some years ago. The people who watch soap operas would understand. The people who know Agnes Nixon would certainly understand.

(Scene fades as the rumpled suit says goodbye, walks out to the elevator and then down into the subway. He goes home and writes his story about Agnes Nixon and flips the page on another day. But it is never that way with Agnes Nixon who, five days a week, with millions as her audience, sits down with a piece of paper, a crackling imagination and that towering interest that she has always had in anything in this world that whispers about life and death, God and man, anything at all that touches all his children.

☙ ❧

Are you able to see Agnes Nixon's unusual career as "holy" human?

Vintage Greeley

Father Andrew Greeley sipped a small bottle of Perrier water, leaned back in his couch in New York's Plaza Hotel and began talking about some of his writing and some of his battles with, and for, the Catholic Church.

Between flights of a whirlwind barnstorming tour promoting his newest book at the time, *Autobiography of a Parish Priest*, Greeley heartily agreed with his publisher that it is at least a venial sin for a writer to covet anonymity, obscurity or the humility of a monk. He also feels it is a grievous offense to be dull. And he had no intention of committing that particular sin.

The controversial Chicago priest, sociologist, best-selling novelist and spurned philanthropist had made headlines earlier in the month when his offer of a million dollar contribution had been turned down by then Chicago Cardinal Joseph Bernardin who apparently didn't like his priests writing steamy, best-selling novels about faith, hope and genitalia.

"My books are theological novels," fumed the famous priest/author who can scribble out at least one book a year and who claimed at the time that he gets most of his ideas while swimming. "My novels are about God's love and how God pursues us with his love all through life. Human eroticism is a very pale imitation of God's love for us and, in that sense, God is a very passionate lover who loves each one of us far more passionately than we could ever love each other."

Not letting go, Greeley continued to talk about sex and the Catholic Church and how most of the Church's pronouncements in recent decades have dealt with sex through its prohibitions against premarital sex, divorce, birth control, extramarital sex, a female priesthood, homosexuality, optional celibacy and, of course, abortion.

"At least," Greeley continued without skipping a beat, "the sex in my novels is always in the context of a human relationship. My novels deal with a love that is dead and is suddenly reborn. But the pronouncements about sex by the Church are always completely isolated from love. I think that the leaders of the Catholic Church are a lot more obsessed with sex than me and my readers." He giggled at the idea of those same leaders reading his comments about their sexual fixations.

Greeley's cantankerously Irish soul then turned its attention to the subject of abortion and the simmering old feud on the subject between Cardinal O'Connor and, at the time, New York Governor Mario Cuomo. "Everybody cuts a compromise on abortion and O'Connor is no exception," Greeley said bluntly. "If O'Connor and his fellow anti-abortion crusaders thought abortion is really as evil as they say it is, then they should spare no effort to defeat all the political candidates. But they don't do that, and they're not ready to go along with the radical right-to-life groups that believe that people who don't oppose abortion are as bad as Hitler. But O'Connor and company aren't ready to go along with that, so they're compromising. So why should they go after people like Cuomo here in New York?

"Secondly, I've known Mario since he was a young lawyer in Queens and Mario Cuomo is a better Catholic than any bishop I know. And you can quote me on that."

And would Father Andrew Greeley last in New York under Cardinal O'Connor? "Well, in Chicago they won't take my money," he laughed, "but they still let me be a priest and let me write. I don't know what would happen to me here in New York, but I think I would have a hard time."

On a roll, Greeley then started elaborating on a number of vintage Greeley opinions that are not ordinarily quoted in your standard Sunday homily. For starters, Greeley said flatly that the single most damaging event in the Catholic Church during his lifetime was Pope Paul VI's encyclical denouncing birth control. "It simply turned off Catholics and drove many of them away from the Church like nothing before or since," he said.

And the most damaging personality in the Church? "Cardinal Ratzinger in the Vatican," he said immediately. "He's a disaster, but he's actually brought a lot of Catholics together simply because they sympathize with Father Charles Curran, Archbishop Hunthausen and others that Cardinal Ratzinger has gone after."

Warming to the subject, he then went on to list what he considered the three biggest scandals in the Catholic Church at the time. Starting with "bad Sunday sermons," he went on to cite the oppression of women in the Church and the $8 billion in law suits that were currently being brought against Catholic priests nationally on charges of child abuse and that, at the time in the mid-80s , were getting little or no attention in the media. "People are no longer afraid to sue the Catholic Church," he noted, years before the events of 2001 blazed across the headlines. The scandal, he clarified quickly, had more to do with the charges of child abuse than with the lawsuits.

And what would Andrew Greeley do if someone called his bluff and he was suddenly pope for a year? "First, I would ordain women as priests," he began with a flourish, savoring the fantasy to the fullest. "And then I would open up the lines of communication within the Church, from top to bottom, all across the board. I would start listening to what the lay people have to say."

In any conversation with the man, it takes less than a minute to realize that Father Andrew Greeley is intensely, unabashedly Irish. ("We talk too much, we tell too many stories and we enjoy life . . . but don't like to admit it.") He is also quite deeply committed to his priesthood and his vows of celibacy which, he said, are absolutely essential to his life and his work. He also has a crusty, enduring fondness for the Church that occasionally manages to slip through the crevices of his goading criticisms of all things hierarchical that tend to hold it back and pull it down.

• "Bishop Mugavero (since deceased) and Bishop Joseph Sullivan over in Brooklyn are great guys and good bishops.

And what I really like about them is that they're both very street-smart."

• "Mother Teresa is a saint and if some American nuns think that she's putting herself on some sort of pedestal in religious life, that's just not true. They're just envious."

• "Pope John Paul II is a very brilliant man but he just doesn't understand the world beyond the Iron Curtain. He doesn't understand the Western world and its Church."

Greeley then emptied the bottle of Perrier and walked over to a table to pick up the book-jacket from one of his novels, *Patience of a Saint*. "It's about an Irish-Catholic reporter," he grinned mischievously, "who is a lousy Catholic, a lousy reporter, a lousy husband and father and a lousy lover who, halfway through the book, becomes a saint. And then there is a little crisis where everyone deserts him."

"So what happens?" the Irish-Catholic reporter asks anxiously.

"You'll have to read the book," the Irish author said with a satisfied laugh, flopping down on the couch.

And then came the nagging, ultimate question that has been on the lips of critics and Greeley groupies alike ever since his first novel, seven best sellers ago, hit the bookstores. The question came slowly, cautiously, poised for a Greeley explosion. How can a good Catholic priest like Father Andrew Greeley write so graphically and in such panting detail about sex and all those lusty, leering assaults on the sixth commandment?

Greeley turned slowly to his visitor and, with the patented Greeley grin and a sly leprechaun wink, purred innocently, "that's my affair."

ॐ

Putting aside Greeley's creative imagination as a novelist, how do you rate him as a Catholic priest?

The Search for Home and Hope

WHEN you walk into the building in lower Manhattan where the small sign at the door says it's the office of the Coalition for the Homeless, you know immediately that you are not walking into the Waldorf Astoria.

The charred steel elevator door is battered and dented and there is only room on it for four people at best, including the young man who opens and closes the door to the elevator that, fortunately, has a climb of only three floors.

And when the door opens on the third floor, there is a mob scene of almost fifty people, men, women and children, all homeless, and all of them sitting there on metal chairs to see one of the staff members about food or medication or a move to still another shelter in the city. "This is the place of last resort," Mary Brosnahan Sullivan, the 42-year-old executive director of the Coalition explains in her office a little later as a large illustration of Jesus looks down from a wall by the window over the inscription, "how can you worship a homeless man on Sunday and ignore one on Monday?"

But on Tuesday or Wednesday or any other day in the week, it is hard to ignore the thousands of homeless men, women and children in the city of New York, with the numbers still climbing every day. And their problems never seem to go away.

On this particular afternoon, Mary Brosnahan Sullivan, whose name is synonymous with the homeless in New York, was obviously upset by a new State Appellate Court ruling that homeless men and women who are repeatedly disruptive can be thrown out of city shelters into the street. "This potentially affects a very large universe of very troubled people," Ms. Sullivan had complained to *The New York Times* a week earlier. "This is a large constellation of single people who are not overtly psychotic. But setting that class aside, there are thousands with borderline personality disorders, long-term depressives and other dysfunctionals that clearly are unable to comply with the highly structured shelter programs. The City has fought for and won the right to throw these people into the streets. But these are the last people you would want on the streets."

"We asked the City if we could develop a shelter of last resort but they were not interested," added Joan Ohlson, the executive director of Urban Pathways which serves homeless single adults. "In the summer, it is not much of a concern. But in the winter, people in the street for a number of days can die."

If the City has fought hard for this ruling, Mary Brosnahan Sullivan has spent well over a decade of her young life fighting for the rights, and lives, of countless homeless people. And she has never been bashful about taking her battles right into City Hall and the courts.

After her 1983 graduation from Notre Dame University, magna cum laude, Ms. Sullivan jumped into politics for a while serving as part of the press team in the Michael Dukakis presidential campaign. A native of Denver and one of eight children, she came to live in New York and was constantly moved by the sight of a dozen homeless men living in a nearby park and having to bathe themselves at a fire hydrant. She then decided to do something with her life besides politics, sent her application to Bob Hayes, one of the founders of the Coalition, and the rest is history.

"They're up against the toughest odds imaginable," she reflected thoughtfully about the homeless. "Some of their spirits are broken but the spirits of many of them shine through. They are fascinating people and somehow, here at the Coalition, there always seem to be angels around helping us."

And those angels were certainly around on September 11th a few years ago when, in the shadows of the Twin Towers and the devastating terrorist attack, she and her staff escaped unharmed but worked day and night in the aftermath distributing food out on the street, finding shelter for the homeless and losing more than a little sleep with no phone service for over two weeks and the heavy, acrid smell of death and destruction filling their lungs.

When asked if she considered herself an especially religious person, Mary Brosnahan Sullivan, a Catholic, said simply, "I consider myself a spiritual person. I believe in the dignity of the person and in his or her basic right to food and a roof over his or her head.

"And I believe in the rights of children to have a place to do their homework and to eat with their family." The Coalition's summer camp for children was due to open in a couple of weeks for about two hundred homeless children who probably never even heard of Mary Brosnahan Sullivan, a young Dorothy Day who is as humble and reticent about her achievements for the homeless in the most boisterous city in the world as she is bold and outspoken in fighting for their rights and lives.

A country girl by nature but a tenacious young woman with as much gritty street smarts as any cop, Mary Brosnahan Sullivan has perhaps the most daunting job in New York with the possible exception of the mayor. And she has always handled it with both ease and grace and, as the *New York Observer* once noted, "if compassion were an industry in New York, Ms. Sullivan would be its chief executive officer."

At the moment, however, she and her Coalition staff of 65 people are embarking on an ambitious new project by opening a new office—the Downtown Center for Non-profits—that will reunite the Coalition's geographically dispersed programs and also provide a home to an array of the city's other non-profit organizations. It will also be at the heart of public education and advocacy efforts concerning the issues of homelessness and affordable housing in New York.

Forced to raise 60% of her multi-million dollar budget through private and corporate donations and foundations while relying on the government for the other 40% of the funds necessary for the Coalition, there isn't much that seems to phase her. If there's anything at all that bothers her, it's missing her train in the evening, arriving home a little later than usual and being shortchanged of all those extra moments with her husband, John, and their 8-month-old son, Quinn.

But for the rest of the day, she and her staff are the heart and soul of eight different programs for the homeless.

These include job readiness and computer training; housing for families living with AIDS; a summer camp; rental assistance; help for the disabled homeless; permanent housing; and even a community voice mail program that connects the homeless with possible jobs, housing and other vital services. But the jewel of all these programs is the Grand Central Food Program, a mobile food program that is staffed by volunteers who serve over 800 hot meals every night at 25 different locations throughout the city.

Mary Brosnahan Sullivan would probably shake her head in amusement at being compared to a young Dorothy Day. Even so, it would be a dream come true for thousands of New York's homeless if someone could convince her that maybe the best solution for homelessness and a lot of other urban problems could come about if Mary Brosnahan Sullivan ever took off the gloves and ran for mayor.

And when someone asked about her plans for the future, a mayoral campaign aside, she smiled, rolled her eyes, and said "every life should have a lot of chapters." Hopefully, there are many more of those chapters left at the Coalition for this energetic, viscerally compassionate young woman whose office walls aren't covered with a bunch of degrees and citations and the kind of preening photographs that are the wallpaper for most politicians and blubbery egos. Instead, there is only this large, striking picture of a homeless Jesus whom she obviously sees everywhere she walks.

☙❧

How is the prevalence of poverty and homelessness a religous matter?

The Golden Boy

YOU know Bob Golden. He's the big guy. The guy with the beard and moustache who has this way of melting into the crowd that is a little unusual for people who are among the true movers and shakers in corporate New York. And for a guy who is right up there in raising money for all kinds of charities in the Catholic Church, he has always been much more comfortable hanging out with his old Brooklyn crowd and guys like Gilhooly and Sullivan and all the others.

And when he is at one of those posh fund-raising dinners at New York's Waldorf Astoria or the Plaza where he has personally raised more than a million dollars for groups like the Catholic Guardian Society or the Cathedral Club, he is much more at ease sitting with his friends at a table in the corner of the ballroom rather than sitting on the dais where most of the politicians and mucky-mucks would give their right arm to be seen and served. And that's only one of the reasons why Robert Charles Golden is so special, so decent a person for someone who has been so hugely successful at anything he has ever touched.

At six feet tall and on the happy side of two hundred pounds, it's not really that hard to spot this actively involved man whether he's sitting behind his desk at The Prudential where he happens to be second in command, on his way to Singapore or Australia on business or sitting in on another committee meeting for still another Thanksgiving drive for several poor families in Brooklyn that invariably gets preference over a night at the Garden and his beloved Rangers.

While the rest of us are always right up there in the front row, front seat, when it comes to taking bows or squeezing our way into the spotlight, Bob Golden always manages to slide into the background, out of the way, as though it was someone else who put together a million dollar event, brought in all his corporate friends to help the Franciscan Sisters of the Poor or whipped up the small, stunning annual saga of him and his friends going

159

around his old Brooklyn neighborhood and quietly putting baskets stuffed with food and money on the doorsteps of families down on their luck.

There are some Catholics who would consider themselves among the Church's elite if they were to be invited into the ranks of the Knights of the Holy Sepulchre as Golden was a few years ago for any number of reasons, not the least of which are his credentials as a devout and very caring Catholic. He is also a Knight of Malta and there are other honors that he has received over the years that are probably stuffed into a drawer someplace in his Staten Island home where he lives with his wife, Maureen, and their two children, Bobby and Kate.

But Golden will tell you that the only badges that are really significant to him are his long-time associations with the Brooklyn Cathedral Club, HeartShare, Xaverian High School and a few other religious and civic groups that know all about Bob Golden, his priorities and his loyalties.

And when he talks about his involvement with all these charities that keep multiplying every year, Golden is typically bread-and-butter honest and direct. "I just feel that we all come to a point in life," he said once in his office, "where you have to give something back. It doesn't make any sense to go through life and not contribute something. It doesn't really take a lot of effort to help other people." Direct and no-frills honest. And throw in humble while you're at it.

Of course, if you're looking for his opinion on some of the parlor game issues that Catholics like to debate, the bearded Bay Ridge native is certainly no slouch. And he has the credentials. With a business MBA from Fordham ("the Jesuits are the ultimate educators"), Golden knows about organization. And he also knows about leadership and loyalties and, conservative without being imperious about all things religious, he will listen and respect the opinions of others without trying to hammer his own ideas into the ground. And when push comes to shove, he's not afraid to express his opinions about his faith and his Church.

• "I don't pretend to be an expert on the American Bishops' Pastoral Letter on the economy but if they're trying to say that an economy that is capitalistic in nature works against the poor, then they're wrong."

• "I think it should be embarrassing to Irish-American politicians that the leaders who are pushing our government to get involved in the Northern Ireland situation are not even Irish but people like Sal Albanese."

• "If it weren't for the people like those in the Catholic Guardian Society who literally give their entire lives for others, we would still have institutions like Willowbrook and we would still have thousands of children lying around helplessly and falling asleep on their food."

"Whatever I've gotten or whatever I am," the 57-year-old executive vice president of The Prudential reflected recently in his New Jersey office, "I've gotten from God. I was raised by two good parents. I've been given a fair amount of intelligence and my childhood growing up in Brooklyn was as happy as it was normal for a kid who liked to play stickball out on 80th Street and work for a merry-go-round in Jersey when I was only in the seventh grade. I have a lot of reasons to give back something." But not nearly as many as those who have plenty of reason to thank him.

So the next time you're at one of those crowded fund-raising dinners in New York or Brooklyn, look for the big guy with the beard sitting off in a corner someplace with all his old Brooklyn guys. Look for the Golden boy. Look for Bobby Golden, corporate honcho, quiet philanthropist, old Brooklyn guy, a decent, decent man. Someone who never forgot who he was, where he came from and why, after all, he is here.

๛

Which associations are you proud to be part of?

An Aging Giant Carries On

HE is 83 going on 23. He is frail and thin because of the cancer in his lymph nodes but, in so many other ways that have nothing to do with his body, Father Jim Sullivan is a stallion. His hearing is bad and he has trouble swallowing because of the radiation but he has never stopped listening to the pulse of his Church, in good times and bad, and has no trouble at all swallowing the wine and wafer every morning at the altar. And when he talks, his voice is barely louder than a whisper but there is thunder in the room when the nouns and verbs are all about the Church and where it has to go.

After 57 years in the priesthood, Father Sullivan is officially retired but don't tell that to the priests and people who know him and marvel at the energy and enthusiasm that are still there after all the years, after all the time he spent writing several books on psychology and spirituality, after twenty years in parishes and another twenty-six years directing the Religious Consultation Center in the Brooklyn Diocese and counseling thousands of priests, nuns and lay people.

He is short and slightly stooped, but when he walks into a room he is the tallest one there because there is a presence and the same kind of quiet magnetism that were there when he first walked into the seminary more than half a century ago. And it is all there in his intellect, his feisty concerns for a Church in troubled waters and his youthfully octogenarian leadership in organizing priests all across the New York metropolitan area into the Voice of the Ordained. But, first and last, there is the kind of quietly unspectacular holiness that sweeps far above and beyond the pious clichés and stammering bromides of others who are simply going with the flow. For a little guy, Father Jim Sullivan somehow stands out in a crowd, head and shoulders over some of those who feel that prophecy and risk are some sort of venial sin.

Sitting in a corner chair in his living room where an old photograph of him and his eight brothers and sisters smiles down from one of the walls, he talked with a visitor about today's Church and about some of the things that must, that will change if the Church is ever to bring closure to the sex abuse scandal that rocked it to the rafters in 2001.

"The core problem in the Church today is the abuse of authority," he began in that soft, straining voice. "And if the priests and people and all the reform groups that have sprung up could join together with the common consensus that this is the central problem, the bishops and all those in authority would have to listen.

"At the moment, the priests and people make up 99.9% of the Church and we don't have a damn thing to say. Vatican II tried to change all that with its decree on the lay apostolate when it proclaimed that the Church is not truly established until there is a laity worthy of the name. But it hasn't happened."

Contrary to the wishful stance of many chanceries that the abuse scandal is over, it is Father Sullivan's contention that the scandal is going to get worse before it gets better. "Right now," he continued, "there is a fair number of priests who are not living a celibate life. And in Africa and South America, for instance, it is wide open. What I'm afraid of is that, when this comes out, the scandal is going to get much worse."

On another subject, it is one of Father Sullivan's unflinching hopes that a time will eventually come in the Church when the priests and people will be able to elect their leaders. "I would like to see the Church follow the example of today's religious orders and the early Church in the selection of our leaders," he began slowly, taking another sip from the glass of water at his side because of the dryness in his throat brought on by the radiation.

"For the first three centuries in the history of the Church, the priests and people elected their bishops, including the bishop of Rome. And today's religious orders still recognize that if a person is in authority too long, he usually becomes a tyrant. So they elect their superiors for only a period of six years. Some of our bishops may be good men but, when they're in for life, there's no motivation not to be authoritarian and opinionated.

"I would like to see our bishops elected for a period of six years, with perhaps an option for another six year period. And again, it could be the same for the pope, elected by the bishops of the entire world, and not just the cardinals, for a period of six years."

A priest of the Brooklyn Diocese for more than half a century, Father Sullivan has a masters degree in counseling and is one of the most respected priests in all New York. Small and almost bone thin, he is somehow six feet tall on those occasions when, for instance, he confronted Brooklyn Bishop Thomas Daily about his ban against his own priests in Voice of the Ordained meeting on church grounds.

"He has lifted the ban against Voice of the Faithful meeting on church property," Father Sullivan said incredulously, his eyes almost as wide as saucers, "but he refuses to allow his own priests to meet. I just don't understand."

Following one of their meetings in the Bishop's office to discuss the ban, Bishop Daily scolded Father Sullivan with an impatient wave of his hand and the peevish words, "don't become a bitter old priest." Months later, the pope accepted the resignation of Bishop Daily who issued a statement that the resignation was on the basis of his 75 years and not on the basis of his presence in Boston before, during and after the abuse scandal.

Father Sullivan coughed again and reached over for the glass of water. "Do you ever ask 'why me, Lord?' when you think about the cancer?" his visitor asked somewhat timidly.

"He's been so good to me all my life," the priest smiled, "I don't even think about it. Even at all those times when I prayed for something and it didn't happen, things always seemed to turn out better than what I had wanted."

Universally liked and respected throughout the entire diocese as not only a brilliant priest but also one of its holiest, Father Sullivan was asked, with one last question, for his idea of holiness. Again, the answer shot back without hesitation.

"Holiness," he said softly, "is simply taking on Jesus Christ—his mindset, his terrific unselfishness and thoughtfulness, his love for people the way Christ loves them. 'Let this mind be in you that is in Jesus Christ.'"

And for anyone who sits down with this frail little giant of a man, there is the unmistakable aura of peace and grace in the room and, in his bright blue twinkling eyes, what must have been the eyes of Christ himself seeing things that the rest of us can't even imagine.

ల్లిస

How does Father Sullivan's description of holiness fit yours?

Matthew, Mark, Luke and Bob

I HAD a page full of questions for Bob Keeler when he met me in *Newsday*'s lobby and then escorted me to his meticulously organized office where a gallery of photos, art work and colorful artifacts blanket every wall.

What's your idea of an ideal parish? What are some of your thoughts about the diocesan press? And what is your impression of Voice of the Faithful? Also, tell me what you think of Pope John Paul II and, while you're at it, what kind of credentials should the next pope have?

The questions were for a story that I was writing about this Pulitzer Prize-winning author who is a member of *Newsday*'s editorial staff, once studied for the priesthood and is as intensely passionate about his scorn for the New York Yankees as he is about his loyalties to Pax Christi and the Catholic Church. I was smart enough to omit any questions about George W. Bush who, in Keeler's eyes, is in a class with the Yankees. "I think that smart bomb is a contradiction in terms," he once said in a speech that spelled out his feelings about war. "Like military intelligence or friendly fire or President Bush."

But before I could get into any of the questions, he handed me a story that he had written for Newsday in 1985 called "What Killed Richie Keeler?" by way of background as to "where I'm coming from."

In the story, Keeler described, in painful detail, how his brother, Richie, had died in 1983 at the age of 36, apparently after being exposed to Agent Orange during the time that he served in Vietnam. Richie had come home from the war in 1968 and Bob Keeler poured out his soul about his brother in that moving *Newsday* story. "Sometimes I think about the cold, snowy day when we buried my brother in the new veterans' cemetery in Calverton," recalled Keeler, also an army veteran.

"When the tape-recorded sounds of taps had stopped in the tent where we gathered in the cold and dampness, a man hand-

ed the folded American flag to my father and said all the pre-
scribed words about how the flag was presented to him from a
grateful country and how Richie had served that country honorably and well. When I think about that day, I wish the country
had served Richie as honorably and as well. And I wondered
whether we'll ever find out why Richie died, before the years had
a chance to bring us close again. I wonder if we'll ever know."

You don't have to roll out a litany of questions to realize that
the world of Bob Keeler has been intimately etched together by
both the people in his life and all the events that have sifted
through that life whether they touch politics, war, religion or
even his beloved baseball. Besides a voracious intellect, there is
also a refreshing candor and a granite arsenal of convictions
whether he's talking about his brother's untimely death, his thirty-five years as a journalist, the Catholic Church or even the
beauty of baseball. He is neither prude nor pollyana and that
comes across flush when he happens to be talking about just
about anything under the sun.

"The ideal parish," began the man who won a Pulitzer Prize
for his *Newsday* story about a Long Island parish called St.
Brigid's, "is a parish that is doing the gospel, talking about the
poor and living out Matthew 25 and Luke 4. And the heart of a
parish is that it is both a Eucharistic parish and a collegial
parish." And in that ideal parish, Keeler, always the baseball fan,
singles out the pastor as "someone who should be a good scout,
seeking out and finding the different gifts in his parishioners.
And he should insist that good preaching should be paramount
in his parish and should always revolve around the gospel and
not just come off the top of a priest's head."

In 2000, Bob Keeler covered the pilgrimage of Pope John Paul
II to the Holy Land and, a year later, he and Paul Moses wrote a
book called *Days of Intense Emotion: Praying with Pope John Paul II
in the Holy Land.* "I remember standing by the Jordan River and
thinking how long it must have taken Jesus to walk all the way

from Galilee to this spot where he was baptized," Keeler reflected, sipping on a can of soda.

"I've always felt that Jesus had a tremendous force of personality and was the kind of person that anyone today would be drawn to immediately. I also feel that he had a lot of patience with the apostles because they just never seemed to get it. They were a constant trial for him.

"I also feel that Jesus never trusted the hierarchy and the Jewish leadership. It's unfortunate that there weren't a few good journalists around in those days because the gospels are really very sketchy. But Jesus certainly wasn't some pastel, pale figure. He was a man with a strong personality and if he had any temptation at all it was to violence because he witnessed, every day, the oppression against the Jews by the Romans."

Some of Keeler's own strong personality, and convictions, come through when he starts talking about some of the Catholic press. "A diocesan newspaper is a contradiction in terms," he said flatly. "It's really a tool of the bishop that ideally is meant to evangelize but its evangelization is actually what the bishop wants to say." With his objectivity and even-handed sense of open, honest, professional journalism, Keeler wouldn't last a week in most diocesan newspapers.

Prior to his appointment to *Newsday's* editorial board, Bob Keeler had covered the religion beat for the newspaper and, aside from the countless stories on all the major religions over the years, he also covered the papal visits to both Denver and New York as well as the 1994 Holocaust Memorial Concert at the Vatican.

Over the years, Keeler has been up close and personal with Pope John Paul II on several occasions and has drawn up his own profile of the man. "A great man," he began, "the pope will probably be remembered in history for his continuing dialogue with the Jewish faith, his major role in the defeat of Communism and the manner in which, with all his travels, he transformed the papacy into a worldwide voice of influence."

But, as an asterisk to all that, Keeler feels that Pope John Paul II has been intransigent on the issue of women's role in the Church, overly consumed with issues of human sexuality from abortion to homosexuality to celibacy and, in his day-to-day philosophy, something of a tyrant with a rigid top-to-bottom concept of authority.

As for the pope's successor, Keeler feels that ideally he should be someone who welcomes the role of women, who would listen more and be receptive to the gifts of the laity, who would speak out forcefully on peace and justice and "have a sense of humor."

It is not easy, in any conversation with Bob Keeler, to peel away the journalist from the historian from the man who is intensely, consummately Catholic and sworn to an ideal of peace etched out by his maker. He knows Scripture, chapter and verse, better than most priests and he is, quotation-by-quotation, knowledgeable of the modern spiritual writers like Richard Rohr and Sister Joan Chittister with whom he is a good friend.

Outspoken and unwavering in his convictions but, with it all, a viscerally gentle, Jesus man, Keeler is also someone who can't tolerate bad, sloppy preaching and, an unreformed perfectionist, is impatient with his own shortcomings having dropped out of Fordham when he thought that only a B+ was on the horizon at the end of the semester.

Garrulous and knowledgeable about anything that happens to be part of the sinew of his life, Bob Keeler is a gifted gift to his craft as a journalist and to his Church because, in everything that he believes, and lives, so intensely and completely, he is both prophet and minister for what he likes to call "the sacrament of truth."

$$\mathrm{C}\!\!\times\!\!\mathrm{O}$$

How do you rate the overall effectiveness of John Paul's papacy?

Lessons from Irene

L ET'S just say that I have never been very comfortable around teachers. And with very good reason.

One of them once had the nerve to threaten me with permanent banishment from his classroom if I dared turn around, one more time, to check the clock at the back of the room during his lecture. Another one once gave me a 15 on a language exam—that's right, 15—and had the audacity to give me an 11 when I took the exam again. And once in grammar school, one of the nuns whacked me hard across the palms with one of those long wooden pointers and then got all upset when the pointer broke across my very red hands. And that is why teachers and classrooms have never been one of my favorite people and places in the world.

But maybe that's why Irene Impellizzeri has always been such a pleasant surprise on the many occasions when I met and talked with her when she was a vice president of the New York City Board of Education. That was before she retired when the Board was dissolved in 2001 and, whether it was in her Brooklyn office at 110 Livingston Street or at one of the many fundraisers that she attended on behalf of the Brooklyn Diocese, it was on those occasions when I always wondered why the Irene Impellizzeris of this world weren't around when I was staring at clocks or getting my hands whomped and whacked.

A smart lady, she has a doctorate from Fordham and a Masters degree from Columbia and a boatload of academic and research achievements that would choke a Jesuit. At one time, she was dean of the School of Education at Brooklyn College and is a certified psychologist from New York State. She is, you might say, a little more than your average nine-to-five teacher. She is a scholar and an academician to the umpteenth degree and had been a Board member of the New York school system where the number of children and working dollars have always been a crisis in progress.

Now ordinarily, it would only be natural to expect that someone who has been a front-seat witness to some of the turmoil that has existed in the school system over the years would be, well, a little jaded, a little frayed around the edges. I know that if I were vice president of the New York City School Board after more than 41 years of teaching, I would be up to here with kids, curriculum and City Hall interference while counting the days until that first pension check fluttered into my chubby little fingers. Which is why no one ever allowed me near a classroom to teach and why Dr. Irene Impellizzeri has always been such a pleasant, almost unreal revelation and a dramatic departure from your career bureaucrat.

In all the times that we've talked over the years, the effort was always there on my part to draw this graying, soft-spoken Brooklyn native into some of the spicier aspects of New York Schools such as drugs in the schoolyard, violence in the corridors and sex education in the curriculum. But she always waltzed blithely through all of it, answering my clumsy questions politely and completely, explaining the Board's efforts in all these areas and never once clubbing me over the head with reams of statistics and numbers and the rest of the stuff that teachers carry around in their trusty little briefcases.

What was always especially disarming, however, was the way Irene Impellizzeri talked, almost wistfully, about children and the life of a teacher. And she did it in a way that was totally genuine, totally spontaneous, totally Irene Impellizzeri, an attractive, introspective woman who is quietly intellectual and obviously as excited by the magic of a child as she was, years ago, when she first walked into a classroom.

"There is such a glorious surprise in each one of them as you watch them develop," she once said with some of the awe still fresh in her eyes. "There is so much richness and so much possibility in each one of them. That's why there is nothing in the world that is more satisfying than teaching. And there's no aspect in any of it that should cause burnout in anyone.

"When you teach, you're dealing with the most complex creature on earth in some of the most complex activities in life outside of loving—teaching and learning. Teaching can never be uninteresting because, through it, we are promoting the development of another human being, and what could possibly be greater than that?" In no way can I imagine the guy who was so upset about the clock saying that.

In all the times that we talked over the years, Dr. Irene Impellizzeri taught and I learned. I learned, for instance, that she was a good friend of Dorothy Day and that she used to hang around the Catholic Worker offices and Friendship House where she used to listen to the poetry of Gerard Manley Hopkins in their backyard. I also learned, from someone else, that when some of the schools in the Ocean Hill-Brownsville school district were blowing sky high some years ago with racial and community tensions, Irene Impellizzeri calmly walked through the corridors of those schools to talk to and reassure the teachers.

I also learned that she enjoys reading theologians like Bernard Lonergan and de Chardin, goes to Mass as often as she can during the week, played the organ as a child in church and is an accomplished musician.

And although she never talked about it, the official bio from the Board of Ed lists the various honors that she has received for her achievements in research, her community work around the city, her contributions to national educational groups and her work with many racial and ethnic groups in prioritizing the life of the child in our society.

"The obligation is there for all of us," she once told me, "to create a society that will provide whatever is necessary for a human being to flourish. It's not easy but we're really only an instrument and a small part of the picture. It's God's show," added the woman who is both a Dame of the Order of Malta and also a Lady of the Order of the Holy Sepulchre, "and we just have to be alert to see what we can do to help youngsters discover and use correctly the creation that God gives us."

There are very few people, in any profession, whose lives reflect, even partially, what all the degrees and plaques and salaries say we are. But Irene Impellizzeri's life, every day and every passing moment, is such a natural, beautiful extension of what she was obviously born to do, and become. To roll back the clouds, to push away the smoke and the despair, to take by the hand any child lucky enough to walk into her life and then, by her commitment to the young and all her gentle, giving impulses, to teach.

ϾჃ

What have you done "to help youngsters discover and use correctly the creation that God gives us"?

Part V

Human and
Holy, Too

Open Letter to a Daughter

January 24, 1976

DEAR Tricia,

On my way out to work this morning, I couldn't help but notice the newspaper clippings of the Patty Hearst verdict that you had cut out of Sunday's papers and left on the bureau. It's probably for your social studies class but I'm sure you're a little curious anyway about her story. I'm sure you've wondered how a pretty 21-year-old girl with every possible advantage could suddenly find herself where she is today.

The last thing that I want to do is preach a sermon or go into some pseudo-psychological X-ray of the Hearst family and why it was that Patty started playing with machine guns. But, at 12 years old, you're still tolerant enough of your father to go along with his quirks so I know you'll read this quickly, and patiently, to its conclusion. If it turns out to be a sermon, so help me, you can have your pick of Carvel's best on Saturday. You may even want to read it to your younger sisters, Kerry and Erin, so they too can shake their little heads about their old man.

But you've always been pretty patient about a lot of things, a cheerfully quiet little redhead who doesn't get into the kind of trouble that your brothers manage. In a word, Tricia, you've always been a little doll and I won't mind, years from now, if you tease me unmercifully about the slobbering mood of this letter.

The trouble is that fathers are always supposed to reflect some strong, square-jawed image to their children and I'm not so sure that's ever really happened. You've heard me start some stupid little arguments with your mother and you've watched me mix a few Manhattans when I should have been fixing a leak or helping out with the homework.

This isn't meant to remind you that I am by no means perfect. That's been a given since the day you were born. Besides, I've noticed you try to hide a smile on all those occasions when I've put my foot in my mouth and then fell all over myself trying to make some dumb excuse to your mother.

But I don't expect you to ever use my shortcomings as an excuse later on when the sun doesn't show up every day. You've got too many good things going for you right now with your mother, your friends, school, your talent and mostly, Tricia, yourself. You have always had things within you that are at once so soft and so strong and so much of yourself, things that I would love to take credit for but really can't.

And that's the point, Tricia. You're at a point in your young life where you should occasionally just stand back and take a good look at some of the things you've done on your own, all by yourself. Some of the fine, tender, beautiful things that you've weaved into the way you think and act and into the person you've already become.

As for your namesake, Patty Hearst, there will, of course, be times in your life when, like her, you will have to make some choices, some of them easy and others hard and troubling and draining. But you will make them, on your own, without us, and I'm sure they'll be all the right choices.

And that's when you will discover how strong you are, how somehow all the choices will be almost automatic because of who you are and what you have become. And when some of those crises rise up and you face them head-on, I'm sure that when you search inside for all the right answers, you will look deep within and see what your mother and I see today, a gentle, sensitive, confidently independent little girl who is loved so much, by so many people for whom Tricia Ryan is a small, special grace in our lives,

Weakness isn't a bad thing sometimes as long as you can recognize it and turn it around and then get on with your life.

Besides, seeing it in someone else (like your old man) gives you a pretty good idea of some of the things that you don't want later on when the world suddenly closes in on you. It's also a pretty good reason to occasionally take inventory of yourself and, in your case, notice how really special you've become, inside and out. And the more you realize this, now and later on, the easier some of those other problems seem to fall into the sand.

There's one other thing. My father never got beyond the beginning of high school and I remember how, growing up, I always figured I was so much smarter than him. After he died, I realized how wrong I had been.

I've had more formal education than you'll probably ever have but the same thing is true now. There are things that I'm still learning about myself and there are things that, without saying a word, you've taught me about myself, and about you and Kerry and Erin and your brothers. And someday, I'm sure you'll discover even more of that wealth that has always been there within you and all of your family.

If you've been patient enough to read this so far without leaving it aside for your dolls or homework, you're probably trying to hide that shy, blue-eyed smile of yours the way you always do and that I hope never deserts that pretty, little face. And someday, later on, when you dig this out of an old shoebox, I won't even mind if you have to wipe away a tear.

Love always,
Dad

❧✄❧

Whose words have helped you to love yourself? Whom have you gifted in this way?

Goodbye, Dear Friend

AT Thanksgiving, I always give thanks for all the wrong reasons. If everything's breaking just right for me, I'm right up there in the first pew thanking God for all the nifty goodies in my life. I'm front and center thanking Jesus for decent health, a great family, enough cash to enjoy life, another year when I've been able to out-run the bills. When things are going well, I'm an absolute saint when it comes to dishing all the right words of thanks to someone up there who probably shakes his head every time I open my mouth.

So thanks for the Giants' big year, God, and you have my undying gratitude for the coffee and newspapers in the morning, television at night, fewer visits to the doctor's office and a wife who still manages to force a smile through it all.

But all the shallow, knee-jerk, thank-you-God stuff went out the window recently when I finally realized that there has always been one thing in my life that I somehow always took for granted, never really appreciated for what it was and rarely ever thanked God for it at Thanksgiving or any other time. That realization hit me like a truck when I heard that Dolores O'Dea had died and I had lost a friend.

For almost forty years, Dolores and her husband, Joe, have been our neighbors across the street and those years have been filled to the brim with so much warmth and pure fun, so much laughter and late-night parties and the bulging scrapbook history of all our kids growing up together, all twelve of them. And Dolores always seemed to be the heart and soul of so much of it as she sat in the kitchen with her cigarettes while the Irish music lilted in from the living room and Joe and I argued long into the night about Kennedy and Nixon, the IRA, Notre Dame and God knows what.

One of the great sadnesses of life is that we never really measure the impact of someone like Dolores O'Dea on our lives until she is gone and the tears that we shed are as much for ourselves as they are for her. You have to realize that Dolores was someone who towered across the neighborhood because of, among other things, her great Bronx sense of humor, the ease with which she sliced through any sham or pretense, the gentle, honest charm that she brought to every moment and to anyone who walked into her life.

But far more than any of that, she was a friend. And that is a word that we use so glibly and so casually as we sometimes count our friends as if they're a parade in the family photo album or so much loose change. But Dolores brought a special dignity and depth to that word because she seemed to understand so well what it really means, what it takes to be a friend. For many of us, however, it sometimes takes a lifetime to realize that, with all the goodies and baubles in our lives, we are totally bankrupt without one friend like Dolores.

With that spontaneous, sparkling-eyed warmth of hers, she was not only a friend but an intimately close part of all our family. Part of every Christmas and First Communion and even the sometimes disappointments that washed in over all our lives as we met over barbeques and Baptisms. Part of the fabric of our corner of the neighborhood that has seen little boys and girls grow up to be young men and women now streaming in to say goodbye to Dolores.

Maybe it's because her death was so terribly sudden and she was still all too young and vivacious to leave us alone with only the tearful memory of her sitting around with us on so many occasions while Joe made the Irish coffee and gave the Irish Rovers another blast at it on the stereo. Whatever it is, we lost a member of the family, a rare and beautiful soul who always brought such soft, resounding, forever grit to that word, friend.

And now, just days after wiping away the tears that were there in church and at the cemetery, I can never again talk about friendship without thinking about Dolores. But hopefully, some day down the line, that friendship will soar again when all of us meet again and, with all those great memories, have a few more laughs together over a cigarette and Joe's great Irish music roaring across the clouds. Another time, another place.

ᥒᥲᥲ

What do you want to say to a dear friend before it's too late?

A Mother's Day Cabbage

I KEEP forgetting that you're 87 and that it's probably a little lonely in your small, three-room apartment up in Inwood when we forget to call or when we rush out, after a visit, with the clumsy excuse that it's a long trip home and the kids will be cranky and I have to get up early in the morning. The four flights of stairs have never made it any easier for you to go out for the few groceries that you nibble on during the week or to go out to Mass on those mornings when the rain takes your breath away or the icy streets have frightened off those who are much younger. I keep forgetting that your small fidgety television set never seems to be working and I'm always promising to take it with me and have it fixed. I keep forgetting, Mom.

But somehow I never forget to tell you about something that is nothing more than a childish boast, about something good that has happened in my life, a raise, a promotion, something that the kids said or did, something that got me a surprise compliment or a pat on the back. I am still the little boy racing home to show you the small gold star that one of the teachers pasted in my composition book.

But I keep forgetting to ask you about your own day and some of the sunsets that you can just glimpse from across the rooftops, about some of the small, simple surprises that still slide in and out of your life along with the special meaning that you have for the people in your life, the people who have always appreciated so much of the luster that has always been part of you but that little children somehow overlook until it is all too late.

Are you still looking in on Aunt Marion after her recent stay at Medical Center? Do you still worry about Mrs. Costello in her apartment downstairs? And do you still think about that terrible day, a few months ago, when you came home to find that your own apartment had been broken into with all the closets ripped open and everything thrown around the floor?

Do the letters from Ireland come as often as they once did from your brothers and cousins that you will probably never see again? So much is happening in your life and I keep forgetting to ask. I keep forgetting to call and talk to you about all those fleeting, forgotten things that seemed so important once, so urgently life and death, and that have now disappeared, as you always said, with time and the grace of God.

But then you always showed us how to laugh at things, to see the humor that is there in all of life even though we didn't succeed as well as you did across a lifetime that had its share of hardship and hard times underneath some of the tears that we somehow never saw.

Because of you, Jim, Mary and I grew up with that wry, mischievous glint that was always there in your pale blue eyes whenever you tried to teach us about a side of life that was at once so momentous and important and, in the same moment, so outrageous and ridiculous and passing. You always revealed the humor of things, the wild, impossible inconsistencies while reminding us always of the constants and those things in life and people that would endure long after all the fluff and pretense had fallen into the sand. And I blame you for all of it. At 87, you have convinced me, over and over, that the elderly have a far better sense of humor and a sharper, more spontaneous wit than some of those who believe that old age will someday curdle them into brooding, wooden statues.

And now, looking back, there are so many things that both of us can laugh about even if, for whatever reason, my eyes tend to get slightly misty when I think about those days. Do you remember, for instance, the Mother's Day in the second grade when I had no money but surprised you with a five-cent head of cabbage? And do you remember the afternoon when you thought I was lost in Central Park and I was home hiding under the bed? And then there was that other afternoon that wasn't very funny when Daddy had to come and pick me up at the 34th Precinct because another kid and I had been arrested for throwing berries at people walking through the park.

And I'm sure you still remember my first night away from home when a reporter banged on the door in the middle of the night because there had been a train wreck and he would need a photograph of your son, Dick, who was among the dead and his newspaper would need it for the early edition. And do you remember how daddy, refusing to believe the news, threw the reporter down the stairs? And do you remember that other terrible morning when the call came from Roosevelt Hospital that daddy had died unexpectedly and how the tears welled up in your eyes in a way that I had never seen before? And all during that day, we talked on end about all those great, gone moments when this frail, skinny little man would take Jim and me and Mary for a walk in Central Park where we would play on the swings and he would sit alone on one of the benches with his Camel cigarettes and about all those other days, long ago, when he would play with his own brothers and sisters in the fields of Carlow.

I keep forgetting that you're 87 and how, even now, you still have a way of teaching your kids, without saying a word, about how to cope and how to laugh and cry at all the right times. About how to see things that are all around us, things that are at once so touching and so tender, so funny and so sad, and always, so very, very human. I keep forgetting how much you have given me since that long-ago moment when I handed you the cabbage and I wasn't sure if you were laughing or crying as you held me tight against your apron and then placed the cabbage, oh so gently, on a shelf in the kitchen right next to the statue of the Sacred Heart, as if it were a bunch of roses.

♾

Whether in person or from afar now is the time to say your thanks. Will you do it today?

The Last Person to Let You Down

SEVERAL years ago at the wake of my wife's mother at Connors Funeral Home in upper Manhattan, my youngest daughter, Erin, who was about five years old at the time, tugged at her mother's sleeve and asked one of life's great unfathomable questions. "Why," she asked ever so innocently, "are people having such a good time? Grandma's dead!"

Perhaps in her young Irish soul, Erin had instinctively assumed that death should be a black and brooding time when people wring their hands and look around dolefully in this sad vale of tears. But alas, without even realizing it, the child was caught up in one of life's richest spiritual experiences, an Irish wake, a farewell with laughter and blather that was light years ahead of Vatican II in its spontaneous, unabashed joy in a time of raw mourning and woe for the rest of the world.

Erin has never forgotten the gales of chatter and back-slapping mirth that rolled across that funeral parlor that night reminding one and all that Anna Rooney, lying there peacefully in repose, was somewhere smiling down on the grand and glorious party that was the Irish way of ushering her into kingdom come.

Now this is one of those timeless ethnic truths that has never been lost on J. Peter Clavin, a consummately cheerful man who has literally grown up around the smell of death and who knows all there is to know about Irish wakes and Italian mourning and the vulnerable chemistry of any family when someone dies.

At 49, Peter Clavin is pushing his way into middle age but those who know him will tell you that this is one guy who has always been stubbornly youthful and enthusiastic about every moment of his life with his wife, Maureen, and their four children. "I probably should have been a sanitation worker and retired early with a nice pension but I love what I'm doing and the people in my life," the 6'4" leprechaun smiles at a visitor.

185

With his upbeat personality and sense of humor, very few people would guess that he is a funeral director—"there are all kinds of fancy titles but I am what I am, an undertaker"—but his education about death, and life, goes all the way back to the time of his father and grandfather who originally founded the Clavin Funeral Home in the Bay Ridge section of Brooklyn more than a century ago in 1886.

It is an education that has come about over the years and some of the more devastating funerals of the very young and those painfully old people who lived alone and, in the end, were mourned only by the priest and Peter Clavin. And if his exposure to too many sad journeys to too many cemeteries over the years ever hardened him in any way, it certainly wasn't there some years ago when he had to read one of the Psalms from Isaiah at his father's funeral.

In all of it, Peter Clavin brings a calming, reassuring air to unasked questions about the thresholds of eternity from all those who walk into his office on 4th Avenue and 78th Street to bury their loved ones. And even while he is always typically easy-going about all the old Digger O'Dell stuff and those dumb old undertaker jokes about being "the last person to let you down," his own sense of humor shines through on those occasions when he will sign off his correspondence to an old friend or a new near-friend with "Eventually yours, Peter Clavin."

All through the years since he took over the family's special calling in 1973, he has been around death more often and more intimately than most priests and ministers. And he has not only handled it with grace and sensitivity, he has added his own special lustre to this awesome, taken-for-granted responsibility that can never be knee-jerk routine or jaded when he stands there with some family at one of the most delicately fragile moments of their lives.

"I listen," he says simply. "I'm there if people need me and I try not to get in the way. It's not an easy time for people but it's a little easier if there's someone there just to listen. There was one time when a guy even started to tell me his confession," he grinned, "but that's not part of the job."

It's probably a good thing for mankind that, as tall as he is with an offensive tackle's build, J. Peter Clavin is such an outgoing, genuinely gregarious man who has always found it very natural hanging out with the handful of old Brooklyn guys that he has known all his life or being part of any crowd that is within hand-shaking distance. If anyone were to guess, they might surmise that Clavin is a guidance counselor, a high school football coach, a social director at some club out in the Hamptons. Funeral director would probably be the last thing they would relate to this incorrigible Brooklynite with the forever smile. It's a nice switch.

As he talked with a visitor, there was a pile of chance-books from the Knights of Columbus and tickets for some charitable fundraiser later in the month. They are only a small clue to his other efforts, for other charities, throughout the year and, in a non-stop profession, there are also his allegiances to other local groups such as the St. Patrick's Society, the Bay Ridge Lions Club, his parish at Our Lady of Angels and the Cathedral Club of Brooklyn where he once served as president.

In a sometimes morose and depressing business, Peter Clavin brings a solid personal presence to a profession that is rarely listed up there with doctors, lawyers, accountants and all the other standard, wannabe plateaus where a Catholic layman can make a dent and a difference.

But there is something unaffectedly honest and caring about the way Peter Clavin perceives the delicately crucial bond that exists at a cemetery grave between those standing there and buried beneath.

There is something that is unrehearsed and genuine about this man who, in one sense, has been close to death all his life and who understands, fairly profoundly, that he has to be a strong, solid bridge for people who, dazed and shattered, are trying to cross the chasm between love and loss, life and death, yesterday and tomorrow.

But there has always been something very hands-on human about this man who seems to understand so practically, and care so deeply, about people by reminding them, without saying a word, that life goes on.

And even those moments when he tries to lighten things up in his letters to his legion of friends with his familiar "Eventually yours," there are those all across Brooklyn who sincerely hope so. And there others who tease him that he stole the phrase from the man upstairs.

$$\mathcal{O}\!\!\times\!\!\mathcal{O}$$

How has the compassion of others touched you at the time of a loved one's death?

Bringing Up Grandpa

WHEN Joseph Matthew Ryan slid into the world, head first, three years ago, as our fourth grandchild, I thought that he took altogether too much attention away from my own birthday which had just passed. And you can be sure I will remind him of that in the years to come.

It's not that I have anything against being a grandfather again and, with Joseph, even a godfather. It's just that I sometimes wonder if these little creatures are perhaps far too perceptive about the old geezer who suddenly appears out of nowhere with his lovely wife to babysit for the weekend, check out the refrigerator and sprawl across the couch.

There was, for instance, the time about three years ago when I was sitting in my son Tom's living room watching a ballgame, not bothering anyone, and suddenly four-year-old Taylor walks in. She just stood there with her hands on her hips and, with a withering frown, directed four freezing words at me: "Why are you here?"

Now I was not really prepared for the kind of deeply philosophical question that she posed and that I have been trying to answer all my life. Nor was I ready for her howls to her mother when she tried, unsuccessfully, to snatch the television remote from my chubby little hand in order to watch some cartoon instead of the Mets.

I've never really been too sure about my role as a grandfather except to show up at christenings and birthdays, watch Connor's Little League games without screaming at the umps, don't act too stupid around the in-laws and help my wife carry in all the stuff from Toys 'R Us where she usually cleans out a few shelves before we visit. When there's a big family gathering at one of my sons' houses, a neighbor or someone's uncle or niece will inevitably come over, introduce themselves, and ask who I am. (Another of those deeply philosophical questions.)

And when I tell them I'm the grandfather, they just smile at me, funny like, with one of those looks like they're patting me on the head and then walk away in search of someone maybe fifty years younger. So I pour myself another drink and look around for the remote.

My wife, the grandmother, keeps saying how tough it is to raise kids today but personally I wouldn't know the difference since she did all the raising. And she really did one hell of a job with our six kids while I used work as a lame excuse to be as far away as possible from all the diapers, homework, Little League, you know what I'm talking about. If she had raised Hitler, he probably would have become a priest or at least spent half his life looking for a cure to cancer.

But I would like to believe that I am not really that useless as the grandfather, some kind of house ornament or token decoration like one of those pink pelicans out on some people's lawns. I would like to think that, years from now, when the grandkids start browsing through some old family photos, they won't automatically ask "who's the old guy and what did he do?"

Maybe just showing up is part of it. Just being there. Because nobody really has to add anything extra to what our kids are doing in raising their own kids today. But my wife is different. She knows just what it's all about being a grandparent and she's very good at it. She dotes on them. She walks to the park with them and helps them make their lunch and gets all bubbly when Connor sits down to play the piano or when Joseph and Casey decide to do the tango. She reads stories to all of them and praises their drawings on the refrigerator and then hisses at me to grow up and give them back the television remote.

On the other hand, I am something of a mystery to our grandchildren, something of a challenge, although there are times when I am convinced they know me like a book and have me pegged perfectly. When Taylor was just beginning to talk, she called my wife Nana but, for some strange, inscrutable reason, instead of Grandpa, she called me Bummer. Everyone else thought it was very cute. But somehow when I looked her in the eye, I had the funny feeling that she knew exactly what she was saying.

Our own children never had a grandfather because both of our fathers had died before we got married. And while our kids never really knew what they missed, there had to be an empty space in their lives because both of our fathers were quiet, gentle men who went out to work every day and loved their families dearly but never lived long enough to enjoy retirement or, more importantly, the soft, innocent look of a little grandchild sizing up the old guy snoozing away on the couch.

Maybe I should get a book and read up on just what it is that grandfathers are supposed to do besides hanging around and watching ballgames and getting on Nana's nerves. But I don't remember reading about any grandfathers in the Bible except maybe those old codgers who were always heaped in there with the lame and the halt.

Maybe it just comes down to acting my age and enjoying whatever years are still left to walk in the park with them and Nana, to sit alone with them and watch Barney, to laugh with them and listen to them say their prayers for Nana and Grandpa and watch them fall asleep. Maybe it comes down to giving Joseph Matthew Ryan a big hug the day he puts his hands on his hips and asks me the ageless question: why are you here? And I can answer him right back with a big, beaming smile, an extra hug and kiss and those three magic words: "I'm the grandfather!"

⊘✕⊙

Reflect and share about your experience of being a grandparent or a grandchild?

A Different Kind of Irish Wake

THEY came with their wives and their white hair and some of the old memories that spilled out across the two days with the same boyish exuberance that was there so long ago, once upon a time. They came with their laughter and tears and, of course, all the old stories, washed and ironed, because Irish wakes demand all the proper equipment and this wake for Kevin McNiff, this last farewell, would demand the very utmost from each of them.

Many of them, like Kevin, were former priests who, some years ago, had put their old calling into a drawer and walked out the door. They have since talked about it among each other over a million times, talked, argued over a beer and cigarette, joked, philosophized, threw it out there on the table one more time and then, shrugging at all the words and time and sameness, got on with their lives.

Kevin had gotten on with so many good moments in the 65 years of his life but then the cancer came and the old left-handed basketball chucker couldn't stand too well any more, couldn't even sit up and talk for too long a time with his wife, Alicia, and their three children. And so, Kevin died on All Souls Day, one day before his birthday, and they came out, priests and priests who had resigned, old classmates from the seminary and old friends from the rectories of Harlem and the South Bronx, an honor guard of solemn men from the Department of Correction where Kevin had been Deputy Commissioner after he left the priesthood, his sisters and two brothers and all the old faces from so many New York neighborhoods that claimed Kevin as their own because he was, in so many ways, so damn ordinary like themselves, and yet. . . .

For years, Kevin and his old classmates had been given their own niche, a little different from others because there was so much talent there and so many other things that couldn't be tagged or labeled and filed away. There was, for instance, that

192

maverick impatience with pretense over passion and that faith that was always so natural and so nervy and profane to all the frustrations. With their earthy vision of the Church, the poor and themselves, they were something of a breed apart because there were things in each of them that didn't come, quiet and orderly, out of a seminary textbook but that somehow soared above the crowd whenever they were together and all the old instincts and ideals whispered again of other times and other hopes and other lapsed, lost pages in time that they would never tear out or forget.

But here they were, together again, for the funeral of a friend. And they were all here, Carway and Lynch and Killion from an era of almost forty years ago. Lehane and Mastrangelo had left the seminary early on but others who had stayed on, like Byrne and Buckley and Gigante, had come out to say their goodbyes and to remember Kevin as a spirit apart wherever he happened to be standing on the altar or around the table with Alicia and their children.

And as all of them crowded into the kitchen and living room back at Kevin's house after the funeral, it was as if nothing had changed from a thousand years ago when they stood around and talked with such intensity about the future and the people they had pledged to serve.

One of the wives said something about the good feeling that is always there when they come together because there is so much honesty and this invincible camaraderie of theirs that never seems to dim. So much casual decency and the unbending conviction that they did indeed share a rare and sometimes painful calling within a Church that is still so often awkward around those who are no longer active priests and still doesn't quite know how to walk and talk with these men, these talented, unusual, forever priests who are "the Church Kevin" for all those graced by his laughter, his humanity and his memory.

It was an Irish wake like few others and a funeral where nobody listened to any of that nonsense about death and the finish line for someone like Kevin McNiff. It was, for everyone there, an early Christmas with its story about the birth of a boy and this small bunch of aging men who, once upon a time, were called to something different in this world and in their Church that the Church Proper may never quite understand. Called to something in their lifetime that, with the memory of Kevin McNiff still burning in their eyes, everyone there understood better than at any other time in their lives.

⸎⸌

Describe some of the feelings that you might expect to find in a parish when a priest or religious leaves?

A Dream Come True—Bar None

I ALWAYS wanted to own a bar.

In fact, when I first got married, it was one of life's first great crises squeezing in on us: the choice to buy a house in the suburbs or invest in Ryan's Bar & Grill which would be a lovely little gold mine somewhere in the city where all my friends could meet regularly to solve all the problems of the western hemisphere. However, all that went flying out the window when my lovely wife became quite obstreperous at the mere mention of my dream saloon. So we bought the house and the bank owned my soul, and wallet, for the next thirty years.

With that settled, I went out and began working for an assortment of bosses, some of them quite good, and the rest (you know who you are) were somewhere from the ghettoes of hell. That's why I have often wondered what would have happened if I had bought the bar and, instead of dealing with the assorted neuroses of a few nut bosses, spent my time satisfying the fierce thirst of my customers and friends. My darling wife, sneering away, never gave it a second thought.

But now Jim, who is one of my sons, has taken that old dream of mine by the lapels and opened another kind of bar, Rudy's Gourmet Coffee and Ice Cream Bar, on Long Island. And John, another son, has quit his own job so that he could work with his brother and I honestly get a little misty when I see how well they are doing, how hard they are working, and how smart they were in deciding to serve cappuccino instead of gin.

The people out in Mattituck are also delighted with the whole idea since Jim, a true entrepreneur, has added something extra to the coffee by having special nights for poetry readings, art shows, chess tournaments, a few bands, PTA meetings and a whole bunch of other events. He's also built an outside patio and added a pool table so that he and John have almost become folk heroes overnight in that small town. The older residents have a place to relax and the young have a place to hang out without getting into trouble while John makes more soup and Jim trains a few part-timers.

But both of them have been blessed with their mother's gentle nature, the tough persistence of their older brother, Tom, and the infectious warmth of Tricia, Kerry and Erin. I'm not sure if I have any of those qualities, or ever did. (It's quite unanimous in the family that I have zero patience, a wired temper, am a little scary behind the wheel of a car and can't remember yesterday. Otherwise, I'm an ascetic.) But naturally, I like to take all the credit for all the good things that have come sailing out of their lives.

But I really envy Jim and John for all the things they've been able to do, on a shoestring, in less than a year. It took a lot of guts to kiss goodbye to corporate America, build something, literally by hand from the ground up, and then throw open the doors to a dream. I don't advertise it, but they both know how proud I am of what they've done and how they've shown, over and over, what's inside each of them. Without even trying, they've brought a close family even closer, with everybody rooting for them, everybody cheering them on every step of the way, everybody enjoying the ride that is really only beginning.

I was raised in the city and was always much closer to saloons than suburbia. So that with the house, I'm still not all that thrilled that I have to cut the grass, take out the garbage, paint the kitchen for the umpteenth time and hope that the next hurricane doesn't blow us into Canada. But even if I had owned a pub, I never would have had that look that I see in my sons' eyes today, that excitement that runs through their veins when they begin each day, their own boss, as they take on the world and everything that goes with it for another day in chasing down their dream. It's got to be a good feeling as the two of them do all the things with their lives that most of us, in the end, are satisfied just to talk about.

Lately when I've been sitting in Rudy's sipping a freebie coffee, I wonder what would have happened if I had to do it all over. The saloon? The house? The forty year commute? The crummy bosses? And then I look over at Jim and John mixing a café latte or talking to a customer and everything fits in perfectly because the two of them finished something that, once upon a time, I only dreamed about. And in taking all the risks and doing all the hard work that went with it, they've reached inside and peeled out all those rare qualities of character and heart that all parents, closing our eyes, only wish for in all our children every moment of our lives.

Ryan's Bar & Grill might have been something special indeed back in one of those old New York neighborhoods but Jim and John have given me something that was the real dream all along.

ᘓᕽᘐ

Share some of the surprising things that your children have accomplished and don't forget to let them know how proud you are of them.

The Old Man

MY old man never took me to a baseball game in his life. I never owned a bicycle or a fishing rod and he never owned a car or a house and he never once took us out to the Hamptons or even down to Rockaway for the summer. And he never doubted that a four-room apartment on Manhattan's West Side was a s good a place as any to raise three kids along with my mother. By today's standards, my old man was pretty ordinary.

He, of course, had his weaknesses. He could never remember all the words to "Kevin Barry" and he liked to wear those wide-brimmed straw hats that always seemed a little too large. He never tasted a martini or whiskey sour in his life but he enjoyed a ball-and-a-beer in the kitchen on Friday nights after work or on Sunday nights when the company came and my aunts and uncles passed around the latest letter from the old country.

Near the end, he had to stop halfway up the block on his way home from the subway because the pains started shooting across his legs after the long day standing around as a security guard at Bell Telephone. But even on his best day, he never weighed more than 130 pounds so that I could put my hand around his wrist and, if his shirt was off, I could count the ribs.

He loved to talk about Ireland on those great and glorious occasions when the Keanes or the Lyngs or Jimmy and Rose Collins would come and sit in the small living room or out in the kitchen and talk endlessly and with sudden bursts of laughter about the tinkers and Mickey Smull and those wonderful mornings on the farms back in County Carlow or County Wexford that they would never see again.

And my old man forgave much too easily. Even the time when the police called him over to the Central Park stationhouse because another kid and I had been picked up for heaving berries at people walking into the park. Even a few times, later on, when I raised my voice to this short, gentle man who could raise his voice with the best of us but rarely raised his hands in anger.

Not even that time, long ago in Ireland, when the parish priest struck my father across the legs with his riding whip because the priest and his horse had to swim across the stream to church because he felt my father and a few people in the IRA blew up a bridge that was always used by a British patrol.

And he never complained about anything. I will always remember how, every morning, he walked down the four flights of stairs and then disappeared down the block with that slow, herky-jerky walk of his and then down into the subway and the job. And he never complained about anything.

He died in Roosevelt Hospital in New York the day after I sat on the side of the bed with him as he smoked a cigarette and after the doctor had assured my mother and me that he was doing wonderfully. I was 21. My father had done everything that he had to do. And he was gone.

Looking back, I don't ever regret that me and my old man never sat in the old Polo Grounds together or never had a chance to shoot the breeze over a few beers at Callaghan's during the summer. I was into Batman and Superman as a kid and getting into trouble with the Castro kids, and my father's only interest in sports was Joe Louis and listening, by the old Philco, as Billy Conn and Schmeling and Two-ton Tony Galento ran but couldn't hide.

None of us owned bikes then because roller skates were cheaper, and better, especially in the games of street hockey between sewers up on 85th Street outside the convent. And if we wanted a pool, there were always the public pools at Highbridge or the Miramar or, if no one was looking, the East River. And we never needed a car because the subway and old trolleys were right there to take us to Coney Island or out to South Beach.

My old man was a skinny little guy who smoked too much and liked to sit around with his friends and talk about the old country or else go up to the roof, Tar Beach, and just look out across the neighborhood, so very different, so very far from home in Ireland. But he never talked much about any of it. He just went out to work and then on Friday night threw the brown pay envelope on the kitchen table for my mother and never complained when his ankles began to swell and the pauses against a car, halfway up the block, were becoming more frequent. And he never talked about any of it.

I never had a catch with him and he and my mother never ate out and rarely went to the movies. But he understood more about being a good father than any of us will ever find in a textbook or at some liberated PTA meeting. And that's why I don't envy today's young fathers. It's such a different time with so much emphasis on career and money and staying young. It was so much simpler, and safer, back then. And today's fathers are learning that not all of the answers are in bonding or play-dates or quality time, whatever that is. It's all in the eyes. It's all in the way a father can look at his son or daughter and, without saying a word, tell them that they are loved, that they are the most precious beings in the universe, that with just a touch of the hand or an arm around their shoulder, they can take on the world, they are the world for each other.

It's all in the eyes.

Even if, once in a while, I could see something welling up in the corner of my father's eyes with so much affection and love and hope for each one of us.

So much that was always there, so softly and so steadily, and I never had a chance to say thanks.

If you still have the opportunity, don't delay. But remember, it's never too late to express your thanks.

The Birthday Boy

WHEN I celebrate another birthday at the end of this month, I will naturally be quite depressed. You see, when I was younger, I always believed that anyone over fifty was truly a doddering old geezer who cackled a lot and slobbered on his undershirt. And now I can't even remember my fiftieth birthday.

But my family has been most polite and pleasant in the last few years asking me, while rolling their eyes, what I would like for my birthday. And, ever the martyr, I simply reply: peace and quiet.

Of course, they know I am lying through my teeth since they all realize, in their hearts, that I would go into a deep pout if I didn't awake on my birthday to an avalanche of expensive gifts and all kinds of goodies.

In the last couple of years as the fateful day approaches, I play to their dwindling sympathies by turning every conversation to my pacemaker, the monthly explorations in the doctor's office for skin cancer, the cataract operations, the old bypass of a few years ago and the cholesterol count that, until recently, came pretty close to the numbers on a sumo wrestler's scale.

But my wife, bless her heart, simply nods her head, rolls her baby blues again and mumbles something quite sarcastic about the legions of people on the planet who have things a hell of a lot worse. The woman still doesn't understand me, or appreciate me. And that is why I will probably spend this birthday, as always, feeling most sorry for myself while pondering some of the events that, over the years, have built my character so immensely.

May, 1957—After a very forgettable argument with my date (and future wife) over some silliness, I am walking her home late at night and neither of us are talking. Suddenly, as we are crossing the street at Broadway and 207th Street, I blurt out the classic words asking her to marry me and, to my absolute dismay, she immediately fills the night with gales of uncontrollable laughter.

"Yougottabekiddin'!" or words to that effect tripped from her unromantic little mouth as she walked away, still hysterically laughing as, crushed, I trudged into McSherry's alone for some late-night consolation and counseling.

July, 1957—During a non-violent truce with my date (and future wife) I come up with a truly brilliant idea and suggest that we go to church together and light a candle for world peace or something like that. To humor me, or just to shut me up, she agrees. And so we go in, kneel down and just as she is about to say some prayers in the wonderful silence of the darkened church, I lean over and, once again, ask her to marry me. Realizing that my date (and future wife) was quite devout, I was supremely confident that, at the very least, she wouldn't break into convulsions of laughter this time.

But she nodded, smiled, took the ring and bent her head in prayer, no doubt asking the good Lord for God knows what in the life that was now ahead of her with the fool kneeling next to her. I had to call on great reserves of control to keep from blubbering with glee over my great strategy. I should have thought of church the first time. I decided then and there to tell all my desperate bachelor friends about the church approach.

June, 1972—Erin Tracey Ryan, the last of our seven children, wails her way into the world, red hair and all, another little princess who would grow up to be as soft and sweet as the day she was born. And now she is married and out on her own and as close to her brothers and sisters as they are to each other. I should have spent more time in church that day thanking God for all the Erins that would come into our lives instead of plotting how I was going to trap my date (and future wife) with the ring.

June, 1973—I am sitting in the historic City Hall office of City Council President Paul O'Dwyer for an interview for a story in the Sunday *Daily News*. It is the beginning of a friendship that I still count as one of the great blessings of my life because someday, if I ever grow up, I want to be Paul O'Dwyer.

April, 1987—I am wheeled into the operating room to receive my very own pacemaker after all the breathing problems and dizzy spells that had come out of nowhere. The doctor leans over and gives me the great news that I am going to be awake for the whole thing while they cut a hole in my chest and insert some wires and a battery (a trusty Duracell?) near my heart.

Then, a chunky, jolly-looking nun leans over just before the surgery and half-whispers, "you know, you have the kind of face that the nuns probably loved to slap a lot when you were a kid." It was not the kind of bedside support and encouragement that I was expecting. Or maybe it was just her idea of tough love.

February, 1998—I am standing in a mildly crowded subway and suddenly a young woman motions to me and offers me her seat. Obviously, she feels I am quite feeble, decrepit, hung-over or a combination thereof. I refuse her kindness with a wave of my hand and continue to hang on to the pole while people shove their way past as they get on and off the train. The next time someone offers me a seat, I will, in all my feebleness, dive into it.

March, 1998—I am doing nothing so I decide to drop into church, and it isn't even Sunday. It looks good on paper, but I'm figuring that God, no dummy, is also figuring that I'm just cramming for the finals to get on his good side since nobody else is really listening to me. But I'm also hoping that he's a good sport with a big heart so that when the time comes for that last birthday, he'll put a big red bow around what I always wanted at the end: peace and quiet.

ᕕᕗ

Make a timeline of memorable events in your life and consider the gift that it is.

Kerry's Wedding Day

A FUNNY thing happened on the way to my daughter's wedding. I went to the hospital.

Looking back, it wasn't all that funny when the chest pains came early Sunday morning, five days before Kerry's wedding, and my wife drove me to the emergency room at Good Samaritan Hospital. After a few tests, a triple bypass was performed at Long Island Jewish Hospital the day before I was supposed to walk down the aisle for the first time as the father of the bride. The first dance with the bride would have to wait for another time, another place.

Disappointment isn't the strongest word that I can think of to describe my feelings at the time. Anger comes pretty close. So does bitterness and the feeling of being cheated. And a depressed disgust was in there somewhere all during those nine days in two different hospitals. At the same moment when they were toasting the bride and groom, a nurse was placing a cold, wet cloth across my lips in the recovery room.

I have always been very good at feeling sorry for myself at moments like that but fortunately, at that particular moment, I was also feeling very much alive. And slowly the thought began to sink in that, hey, there would be other weddings for Tricia and Erin, other dances with the bride, and I'm sure there'll be an extra bounce in my step down the aisle when that day comes.

And later on, I heard that, during the wedding, one of my neighbors made the remark that the day was a true celebration of life, for two young people coming together forever, and for an old guy lying very much alive in a hospital bed and (if you can believe my neighbor) missed by all his family and friends at the wedding. And it's true. There was never a day when my family (myself included) and friends celebrated life with more heart and soul and some of the sweetest tears on earth.

And this was really nothing new for me. And now suddenly it all seems to be more of a connection than coincidence.

More than fifty years ago, a train carrying me and hundreds of other people crashed into another train just outside of a town called Lackawanna in upstate New York killing more than a dozen people on our train. I escaped with a few stitches on my wrist and elbow and, being a city boy away from home for the first time in my life, thought immediately that we had hit a cow.

Then almost twenty years later, after too much partying in the city, my car swerved off the road into the grass, cut back across three lanes where, miraculously, there weren't other cars roaring by at the time, about three in the morning, and finally screeched to a stop on the other side of the road facing the opposite direction, safe, sound, unscathed, alive. To this day, there is only one word in the English language to describe those unforgettable nightmare moments—miracle.

And finally, there were the chest pains coming out of nowhere that seemed so unfair, coming as they did when I was so looking forward to walking down the aisle with Kerry and smiling out at so many friends and relatives for what should have been the second happiest day of my life. The first came when I waited at the altar rail for Pat to walk down and take my hand. But if the pains hadn't come as they did, tugging and pounding just as the sun was coming up, there might very well have been both a wedding and a funeral.

So why me, God? Why do you keep grabbing me by the shoulder and then pulling me back from the edge? But looking back today at all of it, I don't have any answers. Not the slightest clue. In that same week, two separate plane crashes snuffed out the lives of hundreds of people while, in another part of the country, Walter Payton, a famous football player, died all too young of a lung disease at 45. I don't have any answers for any of it. Never have.

It's stupid to think that God loved me more than any of them, sparing me still more time and allowing me to breathe another day and enjoy some of the wedding cake at the hospital a few days later. Maybe he's just been giving me all these extra reprieves to get my act together. And it's not that God made things any more plausible or clearer some years ago when he took our son, Gary, one day after he was born. And then, a few years later, my mother passed away after 93 years on earth. Did he love one more than the other? Did he love Peter more than Paul? And although I've never really bothered to understand or to look too deeply into all the philosophical niceties, the answer was right there the day I first opened a catechism.

But maybe I've never really been prepared for that first step into the chasm between life and death but somebody surely wanted me to have all these extensions, all these double-over-time opportunities to take another deep breath and look, long and hard, at what I've been given as gifts, all my life, in family and friends and all those others who drift in and out of my life with their own message, their own gifts, their own signature on my life. Family, friends, the mystery of simply being. The face of God in every single day.

I honestly don't have any answers. I never did. Even after those shattering moments after two trains splattered across the tracks or sitting alone in a car, clammy and shaking, when it finally stopped on the side of a highway. Or lying there in an emergency room wondering if I would walk away. But somebody made sure that wedding was so much happier and memorable than anyone had a right to imagine. Something that will always remain with me with so much wonder and emotion and simple thanks until that moment, whenever it is, when he finally comes and takes my hand.

ᥱᴘᤲᥱ

How have your own near death experiences or the loss of a loved one changed you?